TAKE CHARGE OF YOUR LIFE

Take Charge of Your Life

How Not to Be a Victim

Louis Proto

Thorsons
An Imprint of HarperCollins*Publishers*

Thorsons
An Imprint of HarperCollins*Publishers*
77–85 Fulham Palace Road,
Hammersmith, London W6 8JB

Published by Thorsons 1988
This edition 1993
3 5 7 9 10 8 6 4 2

The extract from *Access to Inner Worlds*
by Colin Wilson is reprinted with permission
from Rider & Co. Ltd, London
© Colin Wilson 1983

A catalogue record for this book
is available from the British Library

ISBN 0 7225 2869 8

Phototypeset by Harper Phototypesetters Limited,
Northampton, England
Printed in Great Britain by
HarperCollinsManufacturing Glasgow

Contents

Preface

We cannot take charge of our lives by trying to play out fantasies of omnipotence. What we can do is bring more potency to those areas of our lives which are not going well, where we may be feeling trapped without knowing exactly how or why, much less the way out of the trap. Being in charge is not about obtaining power over other people, but about our own empowerment to live our own lives, which, paradoxically, entails acknowledging our own vulnerability and needs.

Things only have the power over us that we give to them. Nobody can make us victims without our collusion. This book explores the ways in which we give our power away and how to get it back and use it to create the quality of life we want for ourselves. It is dedicated to all those with whom I have worked, and played, over the years, my teachers, clients and friends. I cannot say which of them taught me most about how not to be a victim, and so I thank them all.

Louis Proto
1988

CHAPTER 1

The victim game

This is the excellent foppery of the world, that, when
we are sick in fortune (often the surfeits of our own
behaviour) we make guilty of our disasters the sun,
the moon and the stars.

King Lear (I.ii)

Playing victim is the second most popular pastime in the
world today. The aim of the game is *to avoid taking responsibility for yourself at all costs*. Here's how to play.

Convince yourself that you are powerless

Believe that you had no choice in what is happening
to you.

Play helpless

This is most important. You must tell yourself that there is
absolutely nothing you can do to improve your situation.
Points are scored every time you succeed in convincing
another person that this is in fact so.

Find someone or something to blame

Anyone or anything will do. Here are some popular
choices:

- your husband, wife or lover
- your boss
- your upbringing
- bad luck
- accidents
- the Government
- God (do not confuse these last two).

Complain

Preferably to someone not in a position to help. Score a point for every time you get them to agree that you have been hard done by. When you have mastered the art of complaining you might like to move on to *persistent complaining* (referred to sometimes as *nagging*) and score a bonus.

Victim vocabulary

To help you be a credible victim these phrases should be learned by heart and used as often as possible. They will also help you to recognize fellow victims when you meet them. You can then compete to decide which of you is the greater victim.

'He (she, it, they) made me . . .'
'If you'd had the life I've had . . .'
'If I'd had the opportunities you've had . . .'
'Nobody gives you anything in this life.'
'After all I've done for you . . .'
'With my luck I'm not surprised . . .'
'Isn't it awful the way people . . .'
'I don't know what I've done to deserve this.'
'I suppose I'll just have to put up with it.'

Once you get the feel of the above you can work out your own. The main thing to remember is to *be as pessimistic as you can*. Also, *delivery* is important. If you are to be a convincing victim you must look the part as well: a sad or anxious expression and the odd sigh helps move things along nicely. A point is scored for every person you bring down in the course of the day (a bonus if they were in a good mood before they met you).

The winning game

You win outright every time you succeed in making yourself the focus of a group's total attention by convincing them you are in a desperate situation and then defeat all their attempts to help you. Only when they have finally given up (and this could take a long time) and concede defeat is the game over. You will know that this has happened when a gloomy silence prevails and you experience a glow of triumph.

Useful strategies

'I'm feeling a bit down today...'
An opening gambit whenever somebody asks you how you are. Effective in hooking the empathy and problem-solving mechanism in the other person. It can be a one-off ploy o. an ongoing device (the really expert can make it a way of life). I used it for two years with my analyst. She called it my 'presenting problem', probably because I presented it so often. It works out, however, a lot cheaper to try it on non-analysts.

'You may be right but...'
Essential to master this one or you could come unstuck with someone who *really* wants to help you. Be sure to have done your homework and revised all the counter-arguments to seeing yourself, and life, in a positive way. On *no* account let anything in. If you are to be a viable victim you must maintain your defences at all times.

'Exits'
To be used for escape if the above strategies are not working well. Try to time your exit for maximum dramatic effect, accompanying it with either

- a punch line.
- the Hurt Look (practise this in advance).

The Hurt Look is especially useful if temporarily at a loss for punch lines.

The important thing to remember is that all communication *must* be broken off in some way whenever the other person is disrespectful enough to challenge your victim identity. If 'Exits' is not possible then you have three options if you want to stay in the game:

- get angry
- sulk
- burst into tears.

Use the third one only as a last resort.

The advanced game

When you have mastered the above rules and strategies you are ready to progress to the following more advanced ploys.

Being a martyr

Accept blame, abuse or discrimination passively. Do not stand up for yourself. Turn the other cheek and reflect with relish on how your persecutors will be punished in hell. Essential reading for attaining proficiency: *The Lives of the Saints* (for Catholics) and *Foxe's Book of Martyrs* (for Protestants). This is a long-term strategy and it is regretted that the main prize for winning cannot be awarded in this lifetime.

Making others around you feel guilty

This strategy is so deeply satisfying that it can also be considered something of a consolation prize for being a martyr. If your martyrdom includes isolating yourself from the human race and there is therefore nobody else around try:

Feeling guilty yourself

Try feeling guilty about the following:

- being a bad spouse/lover/parent/son/daughter/friend/ example/influence
- anything you did in the past
- anything you are thinking or feeling now
- being alive.

Putting yourself down

Tell yourself at intervals throughout the day (whenever you remember) how awful you really are. The exact nature of your awfulness is not important. What matters is to keep at it and destroy your confidence totally with a view to ending up acutely depressed.

Worrying yourself sick

This is most easily done by scaring yourself with catastrophic expectations about the future. However, a really good worrier can do wonders with the most unpromising material. Above all, do not seek advice and avoid any form of counselling.

CHAPTER 2

Are you a victim?

Sweet are the uses of adversity,
Which, like the toad, ugly and venomous,
Wears yet a precious jewel in his head.

As You Like It (II.i.)

Do you ever feel. . .

trapped

helpless

worried stiff

at a complete loss about
  what to do

resigned

resentful

furious

ripped off

unheard

unseen

'why me?'

'if only. . .?'

doing more than your
  share

unrewarded

everybody is against
  you

nobody likes you

excluded

under pressure

taken for granted

If you answered 'yes' to any of these, join the human race. But if your answer was something like 'all the time' or 'very often' then you could well be playing the victim game without knowing it. It is not having problems, experiencing discomfort and pain, that makes one a victim. It is how one *sees* them that determines wheather we add, as Freud put it, 'neurotic suffering' to 'ordinary human unhappiness'.

A handicap is not necessarily disabling

Some shining examples of this are those who have managed

not only to cope with handicaps or traumas but have actually triumphed over them. In newspapers and on television almost every day are reported the achievements of often severely handicapped people in sport, for example, or the arts, helping organize charity events or support groups, or simply being an inspiration to the people who look after them. One of the greatest tennis players I ever saw in action on the Centre Court at Wimbledon was a woman who had been crippled by polio as a child – and was left with one leg shorter than the other. In spite of this Doris Hart won tournaments all around the world, including Wimbledon. History records many examples of men and women who have achieved great things in spite of disadvantages that might make the rest of us give up. You will probably already know that Milton was blind, Beethoven was deaf and Elizabeth I was as bald as a billiard ball, but did you also know that:

- Julius Caesar was an epileptic
- Anne Boleyn had a deformed hand
- Nelson suffered from sea-sickness
- Napoleon had abnormally small genitals
- Byron had a club foot
- Queen Victoria was almost a dwarf?

There is hope for us all when we remind ourselves that Mozart was nearly always in the red, and Jung, the pioneering explorer of the Collective Unconscious, had had a nervous breakdown. Even enlightened old Socrates was plagued with a nagging wife!

A handicap is what you make it

Virtually anything can be seen as a handicap and then be blamed for spoiling your life. Personality traits, physical attributes, sexual preferences, not having money, having money.

If you gasped in disbelief at the suggestion that being wealthy could ever be a problem, consider the case of Rebecca. An only child, daughter of a doting multi-millionaire father, Rebecca is used to having everything money can buy. She owns a little mews house in Chelsea with wardrobes crammed with clothes and runs a sports car. She can afford to take off whenever she feels like it: skiing, on safari to Kenya, or, if exhausted by jet-setting, to recuperate at the poolside of her parents' villa near Marbella. Yet boredom and a gnawing sense of futility keeps her from enjoying all this. She wanted to go after a job in publishing but her father will not hear of her working. He wants her to settle down and marry a 'nice Jewish boy' and produce a grandson who will eventually take over his business empire. He vets all her boyfriends and so far has rejected them all because they are not rich enough.

It has got to the stage that whenever Rebecca meets an attractive man she feels she has to establish his financial status before she can allow any relationship to develop. From an early age, too, she has been warned against fortune-hunters, so can never be certain that people are genuine and not just after her money. Outwardly bright and sophisticated, Rebecca is envied by many. Yet in reality she is desperate, lonely and unsure, a poor little rich girl. Judging from the press this would seem to be true also of other, more famous heiresses.

A lot of people think wistfully that their lives would be more beautiful if *they* were more beautiful. One has only to think of the tragedy of Marilyn Monroe to remember that this is not necessarily so.

One of the loneliest people I know is Clare, a stunning and successful model. She has no women friends; either they are threatened by her, competitive or deeply envious. She is sick to death of being seen by men either as a decorative clothes-hanger or as a sexual object. The sort of homely men she would like to get to know either do not approach her because they don't think they stand a chance – or feel they have to go on impressing her to stay in the running. Nobody seems to want to take her at anything more than face value and see that she is in fact an intelligent, warm human being. She really feels a Poor Clare, all dressed up and no-one to go out with.

Handsome men can also be controlled by their own good

looks and become a victim of too many compliments. They can remain narcissistic and shallow Don Juans all their lives, maintaining interest in relationships only so long as they see their own image reflected back in their partner's adoring eyes. Not for them the give and take of more equal relationships of less special people. As soon as the adulation stops, they're off, depriving themselves of the chance of real intimacy. Like Rebecca and Clare, they can never be totally sure they are being loved for themselves.

The biggest problem for people who have relied on good looks alone to get them through life is, of course, getting old. Insecurity tends to set in with the wrinkles and, with it, increasing isolation, for they have never had to learn the vocabulary of vulnerability. The greater the identification with Being Beautiful, the greater the havoc. (For 'Being Beautiful' read also 'Being successful'.) Losing what one has been identified with is painful, and many try to deaden the pain in self-destructive ways like drug and alcohol abuse.

A recurring theme in myths and fairy tales is the gift that blows up in your face like a trick cigar – and makes you a victim. From Icarus to Midas, from Pandora's Box to the Sorcerer's Apprentice, the message is: *it's not what you've got that's the problem – it's knowing how to handle it!*

Beauty, being born into a wealthy family, nobility, a public school education ... things many people envy and think would solve all their problems may bring mixed blessings. A title can be a burden, the family name a straitjacket, the old school tie suffocating. The higher one's social status, the less real freedom one has to be oneself. Just consider all the things that royalty simply cannot do, the trivial things they get criticized for – their latest outfit, the odd spontaneous comment, daring to express a personal opinion. They are not even allowed to look tired (let alone bored) while they are working, lest it is picked up by the TV camera and speculated about in the next day's press ('PRINCESS LOOKS PALE: IS SHE PREGNANT AGAIN?'). Successful politicians risk 'scandalous exposure' in their private lives of what would pass for mere peccadilloes in others, while every 'famous face' has to live with the continual embarrassment of being recognized, or, even worse, not. So, do you still want to be rich and famous?

More people, however, are likely to find themselves victims of stress, tension and fatigue than of *paparazzi*. Stress-related disease is epidemic and the biggest threat to our health today. Workaholics can be persecuted (sometimes literally to death) by more demons than any other type of victim – ambition, insecurity, perfectionism, schedules and (aptly named), deadlines. Trying to lay too many golden eggs can kill the goose. The body may eventually give up having to be in more than one place at the same time and just fall flat on its face with a coronary.

It makes a big difference to your victim status, though, whether one works oneself to death because one enjoys making money, working under pressure, giving a service and having it valued – or because one feels one has to. In the latter case, as well as being even more exhausted, one both lacks any pleasurable sense of achievement and, worse, will probably feel negative, if not persecuted. We shall be exploring in later chapters how one can end up feeling persecuted by almost anything. Here, though, is an example of how we can project persecutory fantasies on other people and then play victim.

Imagined handicaps

Mike came for counselling because he was having a bad time with relationships and was feeling depressed. His lover had left him (he is homosexual) and he was very bitter about this desertion. He had just handed in his notice at the school where he has been teaching for only two terms, because he does not get on with the staff. Mike is idealistic and articulate. He is strongly against any sort of discrimination and, as a student, helped to organize anti-apartheid demonstrations and was a founder member of his college's Gay Society.

At first he had found the other teachers friendly enough, came out about being gay and started to pin up on the staffroom notice-board cuttings of newspaper articles (with his own comments) that he had singled out as homophobic, racist or sexist. Whenever he heard members of the staff discussing AIDS he would be in like a shot, complaining about the 'gutter press' and its unfairness to the gay community etc., etc. As the term wore on he began to feel that he was being ostracized in the staffroom. He became quite paranoid, convinced of their homophobia, and decided he could not go on teaching in a school with so many 'uptight straights'. He told the Head that he would be leaving at the end of the following term and gave as his reason that he was moving out of London.

Some time later he was sitting with his Head of Department discussing how far his classes had got with the exam syllabus. 'Gosh, that's very good,' said the older man. 'That means your replacement will have some time left to do some revision with them. It's a pity you're leaving, we should get better results this year.' This was the chance Mike had been waiting for to play victim and he took it. 'The staff hardly gave me any choice,' he said icily. The other man looked puzzled. 'Well, they're forcing me out, aren't they, because I'm gay?' The department head frowned: 'I'd be very surprised indeed if they did. Several of the women teachers are lesbians and a few of the men are gay. They are discreet and most of us couldn't give a brass farthing anyway. What on earth made you think that?' 'They all stop talking as soon as I try and join in the conversation, nobody wants to do the *Telegraph* crossword with me or go to the pub...'

He could have gone on complaining but he was cut short: 'Oh, now I know what you're on about. Speaking for myself, you know, when I've got a full timetable and 4B are playing up, the last thing I'm in the mood for when I come back to the staffroom is to feel I'm at Speakers' Corner. I want to make a cup of tea, sit down and relax until my next class – or catch up with my marking. After being locked up with those little loonies I need some peace and quiet. You know what you do wrong? You come on too strong. You don't respect other people's space. They're not ostracizing you, they're *avoiding* you because it's impossible to relax when somebody keeps going on about things you don't want to talk about – at least, not all the time. You're always on about the same thing. It gets boring after a while – just like those bloody notices you insist on pinning up!'

Mike didn't like what he heard and when he came for his next counselling session he was still angry. Over the next few weeks however he began to connect what he had been told with the breakdown of his relationships. He was intelligent and honest enough to look at his pattern, how getting close to someone meant for him sharing *everything* with them so relentlessly that eventually the only way they could get some space for themselves was to withdraw from him. Mike's real handicap was his insensitivity, his assumption that because he thought what he was offering was good it would necessarily be received by others as good. He simply force-fed everybody with his ideas and gave them indigestion.

Alan is another case of a man who was oblivious to his real handicap. He has always been self-conscious about his height, being rather shorter than average. This has made him compensate by being more forceful than is sometimes appropriate. A professional tour guide, he was confident that his work was good and therefore was very upset when he received a letter from his tour operator that they would not be employing him for the coming season. No reason was given, and Alan immediately assumed that he was being rejected because of his height.

Storming into the agency's office, he demanded to see the manager responsible for booking the guides. He was allowed in and accused the rather frosty manager of unfair discrimination. But this time he got as good as he gave. 'OK, if you're going to confront me on why you've really been given the boot, it's nothing at all to do with how big you are but how big you *act*. The hostesses have been complaining about how you bully them if the slightest thing goes wrong – coaches being late at the hotel, groups not tipping you enough after a tour and so on. That's not their fault and they've enough to put up with from the punters without being reduced to tears by you. We've got a good bunch of girls working for us this season and we want to keep them. So that's why you're going.'

The real reason why things are not going well for us may not

be what we think. This book is about becoming aware of just
how and why we get into victim traps so we can see what we
can do to get out of them.

CHAPTER 3

Barriers to empowerment

Men at some time are masters of their fates:
The fault, dear Brutus, is not in our stars,
But in ourselves, that we are underlings.

Julius Caesar (I.ii)

Before we can reclaim our power to take charge of our lives, and lay the foundations for satisfaction and quality, we must first of all, like workers on a building site, clear away the accumulated rubbish. The rubbish in this case consists of rigid ways of thinking and of reactions from the past that stop us responding appropriately in the present. Usually, these habits of seeing the world and being in it sound very logical and even virtuous – this is why we took them on board in the first place. They have their pay-offs: they make us feel we are nice people, which is what we have been taught we should try to be. We were rewarded as children for being 'good' (i.e. 'behaving') rather than for being ourselves: natural and spontaneous. Sometimes we may even have been punished for being authentic, expressing ourselves in a way that felt right to us but did not please 'them'.

Unless we were fortunate enough to have enlightened parents or teachers, the message drummed into us by authority figures all the way along the line was *don't please yourself, please us*. In those far-off days we were forced to conform in order to survive, for we were dependent. We feared upsetting our parents, losing their love and support, getting thrown out of class or even school . . . The majority of us learned how to play the game their way to keep out of trouble. But the problem now is that many of us still follow the rules even though the game is over. We are not children any more, yet go on acting as if the disapproval of others would be catastrophic. Here are some common straitjackets from the past, barriers to empowerment.

'I mustn't be selfish'

One of the things that stops many people giving good things to themselves is the idea that in doing so they are somehow being selfish. The money they spend on others, for example, they would never dream of spending on themselves. How many people, I wonder, treat themselves to a birthday present? We will spend a lot of time as well as money finding just the right gift for someone we love – and then, if we need to buy something for ourselves, go for the cheapest brand in the store. We have been conditioned to feel that we have to give only to others, never to ourselves, almost as if we don't matter, don't deserve the good things of life as much as the next person. But, if we are all equally valuable as human beings, we do. 'Love thy neighbour as thyself . . .' Giving to others is beautiful. Think what a nightmarish place this world would be without generous people. But how can you feed others if the cupboard's bare? The more you have, the more you have to share with others. At least you will have a choice. People who can't give to themselves may end up having to beg for what they need.

'My friends won't like me if I change'

On the contrary, they are more likely to start avoiding you if all you ever do is play victim. They will probably be relieved that they are no longer made to feel responsible for solving your problems, and, now that you are not so caught up in yours, they can at last talk about theirs. Unless, of course, they have an investment in your dependence on them. If that's the case, you may have to confront them on this – or find new friends. Anyway, you will be more fun to be with if you are happier with the way your life is going.

'I might have to say "no" to people I love'

True, and they might not like it, but they will respect you for it. They will also be relieved to know that they can trust your 'Yes' and know exactly where they stand with you. Love and obedience are not the same thing. Try to please everyone all the time and you could go mad.

'I don't know how to ask for anything for myself'

Most people don't. Understandably, they don't want to. It's risky. They may show their vulnerability, their neediness, not get what they want, feel rejected. But it's worth making the effort to learn. Asking directly for what we need puts us in touch with ourselves and with others. It is honest and real communication, and courageous. Manipulating others, expecting them to somehow know without being told what we need, is not.

'It's better to give than to receive'

Some people secretly resent their families and friends for taking what they give for granted. They feel they are expected to be always available when needed and that it doesn't always work the other way. Often the truth of the matter is that they simply won't *allow* anyone to give them anything. They are blocked from receiving.

Take Carol, for example, She runs a hairdressing salon with her partner and the customers are always asking for her to do their hair 'because she's such a sweetie. So understanding'. Though still an attractive woman, she is getting anxious that she is in her early forties and unmarried. She hates to think of herself as an ageing spinster. She has had relationships, but she always seems to fall for men who turn out to be married. As she herself wryly puts it, she 'settles for crumbs'. She feels she needs to do something about her weight problem if she is to continue to be attractive to men and tries (unsuccessfully) to diet. Though Carol has a lot of friends she never feels cared for, or supported by them. And after all she does for them ... always totally available, a good listener and advice dispenser when they have problems, an excellent cook and hostess, going to considerable trouble and expense to lay on dinner parties for them. After a day at the salon (and even after her dinner parties) she finds herself eating even though she is not hungry. She ends up after these binges hating herself and depressed about those extra inches on her waistline and hips.

Carol is becoming aware of how she is trapped in a pattern of compulsive feeding of others, 'feeding' not only with food but with professional services and a lot of free counselling as well. She never gets fed herself, feels drained, uncared for, empty inside – and is driven nightly to the fridge to try to fill that emptiness. The connection between feeding and loving is primary. She is getting in touch, too, with how she resents it when she feels 'down' and her friends don't even notice but expect her, as usual, to be there for them and listen to their problems. She is beginning to acknowledge that, not only can she not ask for what she needs, but is also blocked from receiving. She feels uncomfortable accepting invitations, as if it's going to be too much trouble for them to entertain her.

She prefers to have them over to her place. If anyone does manage to overcome her resistance and give her something, straightaway she feels she has to pay them back in some way, to offer them something in return.

Carol's compulsive giving is really a coded distress signal that she wants to be treated in the same way. It is as if she gives to the universe – to people 'out there' – in the hope tht somehow it will come back to her. Her compulsive eating is both an expression of anger (which she turns in on herself) and a way of consoling herself. Carol's problems, with or without the feeding overtones, is a common one with people in the service industries or helping professions. Unless they are careful to replenish themselves outside working hours they risk ending up needier than the clients they serve.

Don't leave me . . .

The basic dread of all human beings is fear of dying. Fear of being abandoned resonates with it. Watch a very small child who has not yet learned that if mother leaves the room she has not gone for ever. The sudden panic, the intensity of the sobbing, the total body reaction . . . it is as if the end of the world has come. And, existentially the child is right: if it were abandoned totally it *would* die. The child cannot support itself. But we can.

Later we shall be exploring other ways in which we disempower ourselves, usually without realizing we are doing it. But the archetypal barrier to our own empowerment is the common ground of all of them: *fear*. Fear of losing love, of being abandoned, of destroying another through our demands.

This vague sense that if we make demands or 'do our own thing' somebody else is likely to get hurt can often be traced back to when we were very young. If our mother appeared vulnerable or unhappy, we might, in our childish omnipotence, have concluded that it was because of us. We were draining her, being too naughty, too demanding. So, dreading that she might die or leave us, we stopped being naughty and making demands and became compliant in order not to drain her further. Some of us are still projecting the Vulnerable Mother on to other people and killing ourselves to keep her alive. We never turn up without a bottle of wine or a bunch of flowers, or feel very apologetic if we do. We will insist on helping with the washing-up after dinner even though the host has explained that the cleaning lady will do it in the morning. We cannot say 'good night' before we have arranged the date of the return dinner we feel compelled to offer. (We make good guests for we will never overstay our welcome for fear of draining those who are feeding us. Just like mother . . .)

People with an extreme need for reparation tend to seek work in one of the helping or healing professions through which they can express it. It is essential that they are aware of their motives for wanting to help others if they are not to become identified with those in their care and allow themselves to be drained by them. These 'wounded healers' need nourishing, too, and must be careful to give it to themselves outside working hours to avert the risk of burn-out or break-down. (It is surely no accident that there is a high suicide rate among doctors and psychiatrists and that quite a few social workers I know suffer from depression).

Our conditioning makes it hard to give to ourselves without being judged selfish or antisocial. We have necessarily been taught that we cannot expect instant gratification and that others have rights. Criminals are perhaps those who didn't really learn the lesson. The rest of us, common or garden neurotics, probably learned it too well. We may have come to associate gratification with guilt and punishment and forget that we, too, as well as our fellow men and women, have the right to be allowed to do what we can to enjoy this life of ours as best we know how. When other people get angry with you simply because you are giving to yourself, or envy you because you are happy, that is their problem, not yours. And perhaps they can learn from you how to give to themselves too. There are enough unhappy people in this world. We do not help the world become a lighter place by choosing not to be happy ourselves. We merely burden it with more unhappy people. *Empowerment is about learning to give to yourself as well as to others.*

CHAPTER 4

Lifelines to empowerment

Our remedies oft in ourselves do lie
Which we ascribe to heaven; the fated sky
Gives us free scope.

All's Well That Ends Well (I.i)

What to do when your life has turned into a nightmare and you are feeling just *awful*? It could be anything: a blazing row (even worse if you remember all the things you *could* have said only after it's too late); accident, illness, pain; financial hardship; the end of a relationship . . . you could be feeling any (or all) of those feelings you ticked in chapter two – or just plain numb. You could of course play the victim game, curse, blame or complain bitterly 'why me?' – and may be you will feel better for a while if you do so and let off a bit of steam. But there is a difference between expressing your emotions, catharting (which can be a safety valve) and allowing whatever it is to ruin your health, peace of mind and relationships. In this chapter we consider ways of viewing the inevitable crises, disappointments and blows that life deals us all from time to time with a view to taking the sting out of them, regaining our equilibrium and learning from what has happened so we don't have to go through the same suffering again and again. Consider the following propositions:

We create our own reality by what we believe to be true

What we consider to be 'reality' is highly subjective: it depends on us. There are as many ways of experiencing what is happening as there are people. The same thing may be happening to different people: their experience of it will vary according to how they perceive the event. For example, a young woman going home from work in the evening rush hour accidentally bumps into a fellow traveller, a young man. How he experiences this depends on his state of mind. He could be in a hurry to catch his train, in which case, for him, the collision is a nuisance and he may well mutter something uncomplimentary to women under his breath. If he is a gentleman he could well feel concern lest she got hurt and ask if she is OK. Yet another young man might well notice that she is an attractive girl and attempt to turn this brief encounter into dalliance by engaging her in conversation. The same event, different experiences. *What we make of what happens depends on us.*

Facts by themselves are neutral. History, for example, is not just mere chronology. It is an attempt to *interpret* the events of the past, and each age comes up with its own way of seeing the past. Historians squabble over the significance of political, economic or social factors in bringing about change; the stature of dead statesmen – a Cromwell or a Stalin – is constantly being re-evaluated. Heroes are created by each generation in its own image, only to be forgotten or even vilified by the next. All history is in fact contemporary history – how we see the past depends on the needs, values and aspirations of the age in which we live. This is true of our own past also. We try to give continuity and meaning to all the things that have happened to us by imposing a pattern, by selecting what fits the pattern we have imposed and filtering out, ignoring, what doesn't. In a sense, what we look back on is fiction. We write our own scripts – and then act them out, making them blueprints for living our lives, saying 'this is me'.

Philosophers try to make sense of the mystery of life by making it a problem to be solved – and, like Nietzsche, can go mad in the attempt. So many philosophies, yet not one has cracked the cosmic nut to everybody's satisfaction. We each of us have our own philosophy, stated or unstated, which will determine our values, our ways of seeing and relating, and there are as many ways of seeing as there are people.

Religions, for all the undoubted consolation they have

brought to true believers, in their attempts to nail Absolute Truth have had to try to stop the Holy Spirit from blowing where it listeth by persecution, Holy Crusades, suppression of ideas, and attempted genocide. There is still no global agreement on who or what God is (or even if He exists) and what He wants from us. Yet the religion we adhere to can transform how we see our fellow men – either as brothers to be loved or as infidels to be destroyed.

Disillusioned with the fragmentation and divisiveness of traditional religious systems, most of us have put our money in the race for certainty on the modern religion of science. But here we find only more uncertainty. If Jung restored the mystery to the human psyche that Freud destroyed, so quantum physics is doing the same to our understanding of the universe. The deeper we go into matter, the more mysterious it becomes. The development of modern science has been through observation, deduction, formulation of 'laws', and then discarding or modifying them in the light of new discoveries. We can never assume that *this* way of seeing reality will not be superseded in the future and found to be partial, or, quite simply, wrong. To be open to new evidence that may mean having to abandon what has hitherto been assumed to be 'the way it is' would therefore seem to be using a scientific approach to living. Yet this is not what most of us do.

Psychologists tell us that perception is selective; we filter out or simply do not see what we are not prepared to see. We think we are being objective; we are not. The human mind has been likened by some contemporary physicists to a programme run on a computer – the body. It makes sense of what is perceived according to what has been fed into it. Quantum physics even suggests, with the participatory anthropic principle, that the observer brings the universe into existence by observing it. In other words, *it is impossible to be purely objective*.

We cannot avoid being subjective, and awareness that this is so is not only conducive to tolerance and humility but also sanity. A schizophrenic or somebody on a bad LSD trip has lost that awareness. So on those occasions when life has become a nightmare, a lifeline to putting some space between you and it is to remind yourself that perhaps *you* are creating that nightmare yourself by your way of seeing what is happening.

We always have a choice

This may be a hard one to accept when we feel trapped and don't know which way to turn. But in fact we choose all the time, if only to do nothing or not to make a choice. We may not be in touch with our choosing, or may be making unconscious choices. The famous 'Freudian slip' is an example of this mechanism where, for example, one might 'accidentally' say or do something quite the opposite of what one intended. It is commonplace for clients to turn up late for a counselling session blaming all sorts of things for not being on time. Usually, on investigation, it will be found that they either didn't really want to come or they are angry at some level with the counsellor and this is a way of punishing him or her. True accidents rarely happen, if at all. It is as if, when we don't make our real feelings conscious they will get expressed in some way, willy-nilly, anyway. People will fall ill opportunely to avoid having to take responsibility for a difficult choice, break their legs to get some other means of support, even, possibly, go mad or die rather than choose to face something too distressing. *The more we make our choices conscious, the less they will control us.*

Habits were originally choices that have become mechanical, things that we chose to learn how to do and now do automatically, like tying our shoelaces in a certain way or parting our hair on one side. We get so used to being or doing things a certain way that we forget that there are other ways we could function and confuse habit with identity. We say things like 'that's not me' or 'I never do things like that.' Because a new way of being or doing feels strange or unfamiliar we assume we are necessarily being inauthentic or phoney rather than, as is in fact the case, trying out new ways of being in the world. In therapy no movement is possible when clients are stuck in self-destructive habits unless they are prepared for change, for different ways of seeing and responding. Their rigidity is their neurosis, and getting to see the choices they in fact have can bring relief and a sense of empowerment. *Victims are those who either are not aware of the choices they have made or of the choices they still have. Taking charge of your life is about being aware of and exercising choice.*

Take responsibility for what you get

The quality of our lives is the sum total of the choices we have made in the past and are making now. Remember, your experience is not what happens but what you make of what happens. The glass before you on the table can be half empty or half full: both are equally true, and which interpretation you choose is up to you. Since feelings arise from ideas, your choice of which idea to entertain about it will result in how you feel about it, perhaps thankful and euphoric – or irritated and deprived.

A crucial step in therapy is when a client starts to see the connection between how they are and what they do and what they are complaining about or suffering from. Remember the case of Mike, the schoolteacher who remained a victim of his turned-off colleagues until he understood that in fact *he* was turning them off by his insensitivity? It is not a question of just switching the blame from others to oneself. It is a matter of taking back one's power to cancel out the effects that are causing one pain and to work for the effects that make for satisfaction and quality in one's life. Taking responsibility for one's own experience is empowering, and any therapy that does not empower is not worth much. The therapist may in the initial stages have to hold, contain, support distressed clients, encourage them to unload their feelings. But ultimately some insight has to be brought to bear on what brought them to the state they are in in the first place. That is if they are eventually going to be able to 'walk on' without the therapist as a crutch or to go on repeating the same pattern over and over again, possibly for the rest of their lives.

Getting somebody to admit the possibility that they had some share in creating a situation that is upsetting them, if only by ignorance, passivity, saying or implying 'yes' when they should have said 'no' (all 'choices') is hard. The degree of the resistance (and often anger) to the notion of taking responsibility is a barometer of the amount of investment they have in remaining a victim. It is admittedly difficult to trace our responsibility for some of the pain life can bring; poverty, deformity, severe loss, calamitous accidents to which apparently they could not possibly have contributed. One would have to have recourse to eastern philosophy and believe in reincarnation to make sense of those under the law of karma, the cosmic law of cause and effect. The latter would go as far as to claim that *nothing* is accidental. The circumstances of our birth, our parents, our bodies – all, according to this philosophy, are the results of choices in past lives. Believing that one is paying off old debts may well be a useful aid to some of us *in extremis*: at least one is doing *something* besides just having a bad time! What we can all do, however, is to monitor our *experience* of what we feel lumbered with and explore what happens if we start choosing to see things in another way. How else could a little crippled American girl have become a Wimbledon champion? *Your life is how you choose to see it.*

Change the inner and the outer follows

Manifestation into the material world works from the inside out. Think of the genesis of a volcanic eruption or of a thunderstorm. The energy has to build up from tenuous beginnings, to gather strength before it has form and volition enough to burst on to the scene. It is the culmination of a process. And this is true of creativity in any form. A painting is the manifestation on canvas of the artist's vision, his ideas and feelings harnessed to the technique that he has acquired. So with music, sculpture, poetry – and our life, which is, after all, the song we sing while we are on this earth – all come from the inside out. We feel according to the way we think; our actions arise from the way we feel. Our behaviour is unlikely to change of its own accord unless we begin to feel differently and we are unlikely to feel differently unless we begin to think differently.

The problem is that we identify with our ideas and feel threatened if they are challenged. We may have lived with them all our lives and take them so much for granted that they feel a part of ourselves. To be asked to change them therefore feels like a violation of our integrity; to have them attacked is as threatening as if we ourselves were being attacked. But an idea is only good if it *works*. The proof of the pudding is in the eating. You may be very attached to a particular pudding, have been making it for years and learned how to do it from your mother way back, but if every time you eat it you get indigestion, if every time you offer it to others they reject it and go elsewhere for nourishment, then perhaps it is time to find a new recipe. If things are not working in your life, if you are constantly having the same sort of problems, then the trouble may well be that it is time to check out your basic assumptions and see whether it is time for revaluation. Because our ideas worked in the past does not necessarily mean that they are appropriate now. Life is about change: situations change, people change, we change. To stay stuck to an idea that has had its day makes us inflexible and more liable therefore to be bruised by the march of time. *Be open to seeing things in a different way if the old way is not working*. A genius is one who can *play* with ideas. Most of us are trapped by them.

Positive energy attracts positive experiences

The sooner we can change from a negative way of seeing what is happening to a more positive one, the sooner any nightmare we are creating will begin to disperse. Conversely the more negativity we feed into a situation the worse it will become for us.

Consider the responses one is likely to get if one leaves the house to go to work in the morning in a good mood. If we our selves are feeling good we will tend to notice only the nice things going on around us and to have pleasant interactions with the people we come in contact with during the day. Either they will respond positively to us, or, if they don't, we won't be brought down by them. On the other hand, go out into the world angry or depressed and your experience will be quite different. We will be 'set' to see only the negative: people either as grumpy as ourselves or irritatingly cheerful, delays, things going wrong . . . it is almost as if the world is our mirror, reflecting back to us where we are at. An angry man is more likely to get involved in a fight or a car crash, a paranoid one to attract muggers. It's the happy ones who are the life and soul of the party – indeed, the only ones who tend to get invited.

The link between negative attitudes and disease is well documented, as are the sometimes startling health improvements that ensue from positive visualization. *Dropping the negative for the positive always changes things for the better.*

Blessings sometimes come in disguise

Occasionally, too, we react negatively to something that in retrospect we may come to see has saved us from something worse. Sometimes *not* having our expectations met may be the best possible thing for us.

There is an old Chinese story about a peasant whose wife gave birth to a crippled son. The villagers gathered to commiserate. 'How unfortunate,' they said. 'You must be so unhappy.' The peasant answered them: 'Wait and see.' Years went by. The boy, unable to help his father in the fields, helped his mother instead at home as best he could and, in the evenings, would sketch and paint the family at dinner, something he loved to do. One day the Emperor decided on a war to stamp out brigands in a neighbouring mountain province and sent officers to recruit soldiers from the village. There was great excitement, with the young men of the village swaggering around displaying their emperor's livery to the giggling admiration of the local girls. A neighbour ran to the peasant's hut and shouted excitedly: 'Look at our brave young men going off to fight. What a shame your son will not be joining them.' The peasant shrugged and replied:

'Wait and see.' Time went by with no news from the battle area. The young man left behind was treated with pity, mixed with contempt, by the village girls. Undisturbed, he continued to help his parents as best he could and to enjoy his painting, which now included landscapes. Soon terrible news arrived. The young men from the village had been ambushed on a mountain pass by the brigands. There were no survivors. The village resounded with the grief of the families of the dead soldiers: the women wailed and tore their hair, the men wept openly for all to see. 'What can we do?' they cried in anguish. 'How can we go on living?' All that the father of the only young man left in the village could offer them for consolation was: 'Wait and see.'

One would wish that the story ended with the crippled young man being appointed court painter to the Chinese Emperor but we are not told whether this happened or not. Everything is possible.

Sometimes calamitous events traumatize us to such an extent that we cannot possibly see how there could be anything creative in them at all. A dashing young Spanish officer had his career both as a potential general and a ladies' man smashed by the cannon ball that shattered his leg at the siege of Pamplona. Long months of agony followed at his father's house, much mental anguish as well as physical pain. Immobilized, bored out of his mind when he started to convalesce, he began to reflect on his life and what it was about, to read the only books in his father's library, simple devotional manuals. A few years later, still crippled but mobile, and after much searching for direction, he founded a religious order that was to spearhead the Catholic Counter-Reformation, spread Christianity to the Far East and play a significant part in education, culture and thought down to our day. It is strange to reflect how the great Jesuit order was blasted into existence by a stray cannon ball . . .

The more we learn to support ourselves, the more in charge of our lives we feel

We saw in the last chapter that the biggest barrier to dropping the victim game is fear of being left alone, without support. This fear dates back to our childhood. Then it was a valid one. It isn't any more. You are stronger than you think. *Now you can support yourself.* Of course, everybody feels they could do with support from time to time, emotional, financial or otherwise. But if we don't get it, although we may feel hurt or let down, we don't cease to exist. If anything, we get stronger by exercising the muscle of self-reliance.

The four lifelines to empowerment are:

awareness of our choices
willingness to take responsibility for the effects of them
intention to create more positive effects in our lives
mobilization of self-support to get what we need.

CHAPTER 5

Getting clear

Cease to lament for that thou canst not help,
And study help for that which thou lament'st.

The Two Gentlemen of Verona (III.i)

The last chapter may perhaps have sparked off some resistance on your part. The ideas expressed there may have smacked of omnipotence or magical thinking, or be seen wryly as counsels of perfection. They are, in fact, the distillation of many hours' experience of analysis and observation, both of my clients' and my own processes over the years, working hypotheses that may well work for you, too, if you are willing to test them out.

Any resistance you may feel to doing this may not arise simply from unwillingness to take responsibility for creating your own experience of what is happening in your life at the moment (though this is of course always possible) or reluctance to scrutinize your basic assumptions about life. It may be that right now you are so overwhelmed by your feelings about what is happening that it is hard enough just to keep going and to cope, let alone distance yourself from the situation and see clearly how to make things better. You could be experiencing shock, panic, rage or despair, for example, and these heavy feelings will need to be worked through first before any insight into what's really going on, let alone what can best be done about it, can be possible.

You may have to rely on others to support you through a difficult time, a doctor or therapist of some kind, or simply family or friends, especially if the help you need is of a practical kind. But sooner or later, when you are strong enough to go it alone again, therapy and counselling have to come to an end. Unless one is permanently crippled, one eventually has to let these crutches go and one has to rely on one's own means of support. And, as we have suggested before, any therapy which has not left one in some way empowered to 'go it alone' has not been worth much. Fritz Perls, one of the founders of Gestalt therapy, went so far as to say that anyone who 'helped' you in any way other than to increase your self-awareness and capacity to help yourself was in fact your enemy, for they were simply 'helping' to make you more 'help-less'. (In fact the helper cannot win: if he succeeds in rescuing the victim from the persecutor, the victim's powerlessness is confirmed; if he fails to help, the victim feels unseen and resentful.) But what to do when you *do* feel helpless? How do you grasp the four Lifelines to Empowerment in real-life situations? How do you mobilize your awareness, responsibility, determination and self-support, and haul yourself out of any victim trap you may have fallen into? You could start by asking yourself the following questions.

What do I really *feel* about this?

Straight away this will ground you again and bring some clarity about what's really going on with *you* whenever you have allowed yourself to be totally sucked in to what's going on 'out there' and lost your own centre. *We disempower ourselves when we lose touch with our true feelings.* Don't confuse thinking with feeling. Many people do. If you ask somebody, 'What do you feel about such and such?' very likely they will tell you what they *think* about it. This is understandable, because our education has for the most part only validated our cleverness at thinking and conceptualizing. Very few of us have been fortunate enough to have received consistent validation while growing up for expressing our true feelings. Quite the contrary; we have been conditioned for conformity, not authenticity. And yet inside all of us there is part of us that remains tuned into what is true, even though we may have lost touch with it by being told so often that we are wrong to feel this way and that we should not trust our gut feelings. This is a mistake, for our gut feelings are usually more on target than our opinions.

So come back into yourself again and try to tune in to what you are feeling at this moment. Try to pinpoint exactly the shade of the feeling by labelling it with a specific name, e.g. 'tired', 'irritable', 'confused', or whatever. If the feeling changes or the label doesn't *exactly* describe the feeling, change it. If you keep at it, zoning in on and staying with your real feelings, you should regain some control, feel less overwhelmed by them. You may also get some surprises. For example, notice how your feelings change as you try to label them. This in itself is a useful thing to know and to remember on any future occasion when we may be unable to handle them. Whatever we experience totally, disappears. It is impossible to stay feeling the same for long unless we keep on refuelling it (resentment, for example). Moreover, suppressing a feeling leaves us with what in Gestalt therapy is called 'unfinished business': the unacknowledged feeling will continue to nag at you or sabotage you in subtle ways. Truth will out – or else . . .

Notice too, how many shades of feeling there are. You may have thought at the start of this focusing exercise, for example, that you were merely 'angry' after a flaming row. Yet allowing yourself to really experience with awareness this energy within you which you call 'anger' might well put you in touch with other feelings mixed in with it: guilt, perhaps at the harsh words from you; fear of the possible damage to your relationship with the person you have quarrelled with; maybe some sadness that things are not going well between you both. It could be anything – possibly even glee that you've at last given somebody a few home truths they needed to hear, or a hint of a giggle as you begin to see the funny side of the argument!

Our feelings are often more complex than we think and the closer we are in touch with them the clearer the direction we get for ourselves and the messages we broadcast to others. We confuse ourselves by assuming we 'should' be feeling such and such and then reacting automatically instead of giving ourselves time to check out what we really feel – and responding from that place. A common example among couples is for one to feel that he or she has to give attention to the other on demand, even if he or she really needs to withdraw and be in his or her own space for a while. This is a sure-fire way to store up resentment that will come out into the open on the next occasion that one wants some attention oneself and is denied it! Another example is to assume that when one is jealous the only choice we have is either to sulk or get angry with one's partner. Yet, if we don't go into reacting automatically in a stereotypical fashion and instead check out what we are really feeling, we might find perhaps that it is more like vulnerability than anger. To share that threatened feeling, instead of blaming, is likely to produce a reassuring response that is more in tune with our needs at such a time than the ping-pong of attack and defence. This brings us to the next question we should ask ourselves when things are getting on top of us.

What do I really need right now in my life?

Getting what we need becomes a lot easier if we are clear what that is, just as, if one knows where one is going, one is more likely to get there by the shortest and most direct route. Losing touch with our real needs leads us astray from the path of true nourishment and growth. We can get lost in a desert of come-ons, dazzled by mirages, chasing will-o'-the-wisps that look good but don't deliver the goods. As often with our feelings, so the needs we assume we have are not always authentic, truly our own, but ones we have been conditioned to think we *should* have. Much of commercial advertising, for example, is geared to persuade our consumer society to think it needs more and more *things* in order to be happy, acceptable, successful, loved, fulfilled. Yet the quality in our lives is more to do with what we are experiencing on the inside than how it looks on the outside. Remember Rebecca, the Jewish princess, and, once again, the tragedy of Marilyn Monroe. We avidly consume all we have been told about what we need to be happy . . . yet still we feel hungry, unsatisfied, hollow. This is because we mistake the symbol for the reality, the menu for the meal. We exhaust ourselves running after success, sex (or used to before AIDS), power, fame, wealth and popularity instead of looking into *why* we hanker after them, what we think they will do for us. But if we can become a little more aware, we will realize our underlying longing for being seen, valued, loved; for security, intimacy, belonging; for a decent standard of living and space to be ourselves. What indeed does it profit man, or woman, to gain the whole world and lose touch with who they really are?

It really is important to be in touch with our emerging needs all the time, otherwise, not only may we miss out, we may also give our power away. We will say 'yes' when we should be saying 'no', or 'no' when we should be saying 'yes', simply because we are not sure what we really need. What, in fact, we often tend to do is to say 'yes' if everyone else is saying 'yes' or expects us to say 'yes'. *If we are not in touch with our own needs we are easily manipulated.*

Equally important is to be able to distinguish between what is nourishing and what is toxic. Just like food. Think what could happen if you swallowed everything that was put before you without tasting and chewing it first, extracting the goodness and discarding the rest. Trust the taste-buds of your own awareness, your gut feelings about what's right for you and what isn't, and you will never go far wrong.

Why am I not getting what I need?

Getting angry, blaming or withdrawing, and all the other ways in which we instinctively try to protect our own vulnerability or to punish those who we think are trying to hurt us may well be on the surface. Beneath this surface there are usually needs which are not being met – which is why we rage, blame or withdraw in the first place. Once we get in touch with what it is we really need we should ask ourselves why it's not happening. Here's a check-list.

● **Have I asked for what I need?**

You might have to, or even shout if you are not being heard. Check if you have any aversion to asking for anything.

● **Do I assume others should know what I need?**

Don't. You are no longer an infant. Also, do you know anyone who is a mind reader?

● **Why aren't they delivering the goods?**

Perhaps you are giving double messages. Or perhaps they choose not to. That is their freedom.

● **Are my expectations too high?**

Having any expectations at all is asking for disappointment. Others are not in this world to meet our expectations.

● **Are they unwilling/unable to meet my demands?**

Possibly. If so, how come you cannot accept this?

● **Am I open to receiving?**

Are you willing to be treated, to relinquish the power-place of the giver, and to allow others to feel they have something of value to offer you?

● **Do I feel I deserve to get what I need?**

It's important to check this out quite thoroughly or there is no way you will get what you need. Even if you do, you'll probably throw it right back out of guilt.

What has to change for me to get what I need?

You don't get much choice on this one. As the song goes, something's gotta give – and it's gotta be either them or you. Either circumstances, luck, people, things outside yourself, have to change – or you do. It is easier to change yourself than to change other people (assuming that's ever possible anyway). Lady Luck is 'a fickle jade', life is notorious for doing its own thing regardless. And even if we do have to change the outer circumstances, for example, leaving our partner or our job because they have become unbearable, it's always got to be preceded by some change in ourselves first, to summon the courage to make the decision. We may have to reconsider our priorities, to risk security or popularity, face our fear of screwing everything up, possibly ending up with nothing – no relationship, no job, no money. Reassessing situations when it is imperative we do so takes either honesty or desperation. Getting ourselves out of a rut always takes guts. It is usually easier to put up with an ongoing situation that we have become used to than to make radical changes. I know couples who stay in a relationship even though they have a horrible time together. They prefer the hell of being together to facing a life alone. The future is always an unknown quantity; the past is at least familiar.

Don't expect to get support for deciding to do your own thing or for not meeting other people's expectations. Even those who care most for us often feel threatened by changes we are trying to make in our lives. They want us to stay the same. They, too, are afraid of change. And if, on the other hand, they *don't* really care for you, what have you got to lose, except your status as victim? Remember that persecutors and victims need each other. The most important thing that you might have to change is collusion in the Victim Game with your persecutor or persecutors – whatever he, she, it or they are thought to be.

What did *I* contribute to creating this situation?

Sometimes the answer to this question will be painfully obvious. It is easy to be wise after the event, to see where we went wrong. But at least this is better than not wising up at all to whatever responsibility one had in creating any unpleasant situation one finds oneself in. And in some way it helps us to admit we were at fault. It (whatever it is) may still smart, but it doesn't disempower. It is a mark of intelligence to learn from our mistakes. The mistake might have been some lack of awareness on our part: insensitivity that led to a confrontation, perhaps; misunderstanding instructions that led to lines getting crossed and total confusion; being ripped off because we were too naïve; falling ill because we were not taking enough care of ourselves. To own our responsibility in contributing to our own misery means at least that we were not victims, and reminds us that what we can cause we can choose not to cause again in future. And if we can steel ourselves to admit to having been unaware, it could also be a relief for those close to us not to have to feel guilty or be as perfect as we are.

Often, though, there seems to be no connection at all between what is happening and anything we ourselves did. Maybe, in fact, it wasn't anything we did but rather where we were at. When things have gone wrong it is worthwhile trying to cast our minds back to what was going on with us at the time, what we were thinking, feeling, expecting or wanting to happen. We have suggested how thought forms and feelings, given enough attention and energy, can eventually manifest themselves on the material plane, just as, for example, a carpenter translates his idea of a table into the physical reality of one, an artist translates his ideas into a painting, or a writer translates his into a book. In the same way, we can attract experiences into our lives, translate ideas into reality by consciously or unconsciously brooding on them. It is as if we invite them into objective existence. Muggers zone in on paranoid people in the same way that predators in the wild single out the most vulnerable animal in the stampeding herd, or that dogs can smell fear. Recently, a friend was mugged twice within five weeks. The first time was late at night on the way home from the theatre. When she was telling me the story she said 'I knew something like this was going to happen, I just felt it.' I asked her why she hadn't taken a cab if that were the case. 'I wanted to save money,' she replied, a little sheepishly. Just over a month later the same thing happened, this time in the afternoon. In the meantime she had been taking cabs home at night and had become much more aware of what can happen to women (and indeed men) walking in the streets alone late at night in a big city. On the second occasion she had been walking down the street where she lived. There was nobody else around except a tall man walking towards her on the same side. Something inside her flashed a warning but she kept on walking. As she passed him he suddenly made a grab for her bag. In the struggle that followed she ended up on the ground, still clinging to the bag, furious, shouting 'No, not again!' The mugger produced a flick-knife, cut the straps of her bag and ran off with it. She told me how she remembered feeling surprised at how angry she was while it was happening, rather than afraid. On reflection she realized that she was angry with herself for yet again ignoring her intuition and vowed that in future she would always trust these warnings from within. I hope she does. They might save her life one day.

Setting goals

Now you have got back in touch with your feelings and needs and have some awareness, too, of how you got into this mess in the first place and have learned something from it, it is time to start considering what you can do to improve your situation. There is (as always) much truth in proverbs and where there is a will there is always a way. *There is always something you can do to make things better than they are*. All you need is:

- to be clear what your goal is
- to focus your attention and energy into attaining it
- to have faith that you can do it
- to mobilize all the support you need.

If you are really clear about what you need then the goals, i.e., what will satisfy those needs, will usually be obvious. If they are not, then a good way to clarify things is to imagine that you have already got what you need, are already where you would like to be. Imagine that all your problems are behind you. How would that feel? Ignore what your mind is saying ('this is unrealistic, crazy, useless, a waste of time etc., etc.') and just allow yourself the luxury of a little reverie, a day-dream. How would it feel to have things going the way you wanted them to go for a change? Allow yourself to enjoy whatever feelings are associated with the satisfaction of your needs, relief, joy, gratitude, whatever. After a little while try to visualize the picture that goes with these feelings in as much detail as you can. Where are you? Who, if anyone, is with you? What is happening in this home-movie you are producing in your imagination? How are your circumstances different from what they are now? What has changed? Visualizations are a powerful tool that can be used to activate the forces that work for us in our unconscious. In later chapters we shall be using them for healing purposes, or for helping us to manifest what we want in our lives. Here we are using a visualization to tap into information as to what course of action we need to take, from a deeper source than the superficial level that is our everyday consciousness. *There is, in all of us, a part that always knows what is best for us.* Learning to listen to this part and to trust it develops our intuition more and more until we instinctively sense which way we need to go. The result of our conditioning has been to atrophy this function in most people, for we have been taught to listen to everything and everyone but ourselves. Yet we never lose it; it is immensely patient with us and is always trying to guide us, as in dreams, for example.

The unconscious is always creative and full of surprises. It is good at resolving the tension of two opposites by coming up with what Jung called the 'higher third' and Hegel the 'synthesis' between 'thesis' and 'antithesis', i.e., a way out of a problem that you never thought of before. One never really solves an existential problem – either one merely compromises or transcends it, comes up with some new way of seeing that dissolves it. This is what lateral thinking is about. So be ready to consider anything unexpected (and even, perhaps, startling) that figures in your visualization. It may be a clue, pointing in the direction that you need to start moving in. Also, be prepared to kill any sacred cows, to drop any attachments that are in your way. Nothing is sacred, or everything is. Choose your gods wisely if *you* don't want to end up a poor cow.

The goals you choose to set for yourself can be either long-term or short-term, or both. Better to have just one, and to focus on that than to have several. If you do have more than one, be clear as to which is the most important, the most pressing. Getting one's priorities right always makes things run smoother – and that applies to living just as to everything else.

Keep your goal constantly with you. You can do this in a number of ways, including literally. Write it down on a small card and carry it with you in your pocket or handbag. Fish it out at least once a day to remind yourself of your focus. Gurdjieff used to recommend to his students that, having found their focus, they should write it in block capitals on a large poster and keep it in their bedroom on the wall facing the bed, to remind them. It would be the first thing they would see on awakening. He would warn them of our natural tendency to forget, to get discouraged if we are not immediately successful, for energy to start going out of trying to attain the goal. Don't let this happen. If you really are determined to make it, you will. It's a question of how much energy you are willing to put into it. And faith that you can achieve it.

Whether or not faith can actually move mountains, it will certainly move you in the direction you want to go. Be watchful for any influences that sap energy and confidence away from you achieving your goals, whether from inside you or outside you. Avoid discussing what you are working for with pessimistic friends who might make you doubt your own capacities or the feasibility of what you are setting up. If confidence is what you lack, encourage yourself with affirmations, positive statements that will counteract any negative tapes you may be carrying around in your mind-computer. These are best done when your mind is not very active and is at its most receptive, i.e. immediately upon waking in the morning and just before you sink into slumber at night. Try to pinpoint exactly what the lack of confidence is about – then make up a sentence which says exactly the opposite of what you have been telling yourself. Here are a few examples to start you off.

Negative statement	Positive affirmation
I'll never be able to make it	I can take this in my stride
This is too hard for me	It's a piece of cake
I'm going to fail	I will reach my goal
It's just not happening	It is happening and will manifest itself soon

As well as focusing and encouraging yourself, mobilize all the necessary resources to attain the goal you have set yourself. Once life registers that you mean business, and on condition that what you are aiming for is humanly possible, in your best interests and harms nobody else, it will support you. You will find that small miracles start to happen, surprising coincidences, inspiration as to what you need to do next. If we are clear about what we want and are willing to put energy into getting it, the sky's the limit.

In the following chapters we shall be applying these principles to the areas of our lives where we are most likely to be experiencing confusion and powerlessness.

CHAPTER 6

Taking charge of your health

Self-love, my liege, is not so vile a sin,
As self-neglecting.

King Henry V (II.iv)

What do we need for quality in life? Whatever else we might want to include, we would probably all want to have the following:

- Good health
- Nourishing relationships
- A decent standard of living
- Inner peace.

We have to give attention to all of them, keep them all up to scratch. It is rather like juggling; let any one of them slip and you're in trouble. In the chapters that follow we shall be looking at how we can take charge in these four areas so crucial to our sense of well-being, so that life is worth living.

Let us start with health, for it is perhaps the area we most take for granted. Liberace was almost certainly not the first multi-millionaire to remark wistfully, just before he died, that all his possessions seemed worthless, now that he was seriously ill, compared to the jewel of good health. It is an area, too, where we feel most at the mercy of the 'experts' whom we consult to tell us what is going wrong with our bodies (often in language we can't understand) and to put them right again, rather as we go to the car mechanic to get our car back on the road. We can feel disempowered by anxiety about our health, suffering from illness or pain, helpless or dependent on others to look after us. Alas, the 'experts' cannot always deliver the goods. We should of course consult them when feeling ill, and it is assumed throughout this chapter that the reader will do so as the first resort if at all anxious about health matters. But, often, for all the effective things modern medicine undoubtedly can do to help us, sometimes it is powerless. There are some conditions for which drugs or surgery are inappropriate, much 'dis-ease' that eludes diagnosis, or for which there is no known cure, chronic conditions that won't get any better. Not only that, but there is growing awareness and concern at the sheer number of drugs being prescribed, their side-effects, ranging from inconvenient through alarming to disastrous, and, in some cases, to addiction. It is probable that, as well as the fine work being done by surgeons in saving lives, much of the surgery performed routinely today is unnecessary, while there is no guarantee that it will do any good anyway. Add to the growing awareness of the limitations of orthodox medicine the crowded surgeries, the long waiting lists for admission to hospitals, and one can understand why so many people became interested in creating a more healthy lifestyle, even before the spectre of AIDS appeared to make looking after yourself literally a matter of life and death.

We now have an abundance of books on healthy eating, diets, food additives, supplements, allergies, slimming, workouts, yoga, alternative therapies, how to cure this or that – even on safe sex. Never before in history have so many people been so health conscious or so well-informed about health. Are you one of them? Check whether you are doing all the basic things you should be doing to stay healthy.

Are you looking after your body?

Are you ...

ensuring that you're getting enough proteins, vitamins
    and minerals
checking supermarket foods for E numbers
    (additives)

cutting out junk foods, e.g. sugar, cakes, 'fast foods', ice cream, sweets

eating fish in preference to meat

grilling rather than frying

cooking without salt

including raw or lightly cooked vegetables with every meal

eating more salads and fruit, nuts and seeds, pulses

using only polyunsaturated vegetable oils

eating only a small amount of eggs, butter, hard cheeses, cream

choosing stoneground wholemeal bread instead of white

eating brown rice instead of white

including more fibre in your diet

eating slowly, chewing your food and allowing enough time to digest it

occasionally going on a cleansing diet

cutting out (or down on) alcohol, coffee, tobacco, and other drugs?

Do you . . .

take enough exercise

get enough sleep

give yourself periods during the day to unwind

take at least one holiday a year?

Are you . . .

monogamous or

limiting the number of your sexual partners *and*

indulging only in safe sex?

The panic over AIDS has been due partly to paranoia induced by the media or apocalyptic pronouncements which, confusing hygiene with morality, have reactivated the sexual guilt that seemed in the swinging sixties and seventies to have disappeared forever. Even more so, however, it is perhaps due to fright at the burden of having to take responsibility for their own health (and indeed survival) that is now being thrust squarely back upon vast numbers of people who have not been accustomed to doing so. This is not all to the bad. AIDS, for all the misery it has brought to some and anxiety to many, is proving our teacher. *The lesson AIDS is teaching us is twofold: the importance of our immune system in preventing illness and the ways in which it can be undermined or strengthened.* Prevention is better than cure, and, in the absence of any cure, it becomes the only option open to us.

Building up resistance to, rather than relying on antibiotics after, *any* type of infection is the message and, indeed, the effect of too many antibiotics or steroids is to weaken our own immune systems. This new awareness may well lead to a generally higher standard of health as well as saving lives in the future, not only from AIDS, but from *any* disease.

Modern allopathic medicine uses drugs and surgery to 'cure' symptoms which, following Pasteur, it sees as being caused by external events, for example, the invasion of bacteria. 'Alternative' medicine sees the body as self-healing: the cure comes from within and symptoms are a sign of the defence system at work. It is not the practitioner but Nature that does the healing, given half a chance, with sound diet and rest, ridding the body of toxins and the mind of stress.

What a homoeopath or an acupuncturist can do is to boost and balance the body's own vital force so that it gets more 'juice' to right itself. Here are some other ways in which you can do this for yourself (assuming once again, that you have first consulted a qualified medical or alternative practitioner if you are at all anxious about your health).

Foods that boost your immune system

(NOTE: Immunity is weakened by too much sugar and too much cereal and other carbohydrate foods. Too much alcohol reduces B-cell activity and smoking destroys vitamin C.)

Proteins

Meat, fish, poultry, eggs, milk, cheese, yoghurt, pulses (peas, beans, lentils), whole grains (e.g. brown rice), nuts.

Vitamins

The most important is Vitamin C, but A, B, and E also enhance immunity. They are present in the following foods:

Vitamin C

Green, leafy vegetables (especially peppers and watercress), potatoes, fruit (especially citrus fruits, strawberries, black-currants, rosehips), sprouting grains and seeds, fruit and vegetable juices. Vitamin C in high doses can abort a cold, helps wounds heal faster and speeds convalescence.

Vitamin A

The richest sources are halibut and cod liver oil, liver and carrots. Also present in green, leafy vegetables (especially watercress, spinach, cabbage, lettuce, broccoli), fish, red and yellow fruits (e.g. peaches, apricots, water-melon). Munch one carrot a day and you'll never be short of vitamin A. It contains nearly seven times the recommended daily intake.

Vitamin B

The most complex of the vitamins. It is water-soluble, cannot be stored in the body and therefore has to be supplied every day. Most of the B vitamins are concerned with the body's ability to convert the food we eat into energy and are essential for maintaining the nervous system, combating fatigue and stress, and for a sense of well-being.

B2, B5, B6 and folic acid enhance immunity. They are present in the following foods:

B2 (Riboflavin)

Meat, soya beans, eggs, vegetables, poultry, milk, cheese, yeast, wheatgerm (Note: this vitamin is destroyed by sunlight).

B5 (Pantothenic Acid)

Liver, eggs yolks, leafy green vegetables, whole milk, whole grains, brewer's yeast, wheatgerm, soy beans, sprouting grains and seeds, sesame and sunflower seeds, peanuts.

B6 (Pyridoxone)
Also helps to maintain good circulation and to prevent heart disease. Meat, fish, egg yolks, whole grains, green vegetables, avocados, dried fruits, sprouting seeds and grains, brewer's yeast, wheatgerm, molasses, bananas (one large banana supplies a third of daily needs).

Folic Acid (Folate)
Signs of deficiency: anaemia, weakness, fatigue, depression. Spinach, endive, brussels sprouts, broccoli, lentils, turnips, nuts, whole grains, soya beans, brewer's yeast, potatoes (a 6 oz portion provides half the recommended daily intake).

Vitamin E
The 'wonder vitamin' associated with maintaining youth and libido. Wheatgerm, cold-pressed oils (eg sunflower oil, unhydrogenated margarine), parsley, broccoli, spinach, asparagus, almonds, walnuts, seeds, whole grain cereals (one 4 oz serving of muesli provides a quarter of the RDA).

Minerals

The most important is the trace element selenium, present in whole grains, wheat germ, meat, brewer's yeast, milk, vegetables, garlic, fruits, nuts. Other minerals that help strengthen the immune system are iron, zinc, calcium, magnesium, iodine and copper. If you eat plenty of the foods listed above under vitamins you should be getting enough of these.

When to take extra vitamins or food supplements

By now it should be clear which foods are best for us. If you stick to these and have not let yourself get run down you should be getting the nourishment your body needs. One can overdose or create imbalance by taking extra vitamin supplements (except with Vitamin C). However, your diet may need supplementing temporarily if you are:

- ill or convalescent (all vitamins and especially C in high doses)
- a heavy smoker (vitamin C)
- a heavy drinker (vitamins B1 and C)
- strictly vegetarian (vitamin B12, found only in animal foods)
- under stress (B complex, especially B5, C and E. Also, liver is rich in anti-stress factors)
- suffering from pre-menstrual tension (up to 50 mg B6, taken daily for a fortnight before the start of the period)
- using contraceptive pills (vitamin C)
- lacking sexual energy (ginseng, vitamin E).

Listening to your body

Wise eating is our first line of defence, not only against AIDS, but against disease in general. But as well as strengthening the immune system, we have to avoid putting our bodies under stress. The second line of defence is our own sensitivity to when we are doing so. Trust your intuition. If you are well you will *feel* well. But we should be alert to the first subtle complaints from our bodies (e.g. discomfort, fatigue, depression, feeling vaguely 'off') that we are overdoing things. It may be that we are working too hard, or playing too hard, over-eating, or not getting enough sleep. We may get away with it for so long, depending on the strength of our constitution, but we are asking for trouble. If *we* don't take responsibility for living in harmony with our own rhythm, correcting our own over-indulgences, restoring our vital energy, then our body has to take over the job for us to ensure our survival. It will do this in any number of ways: they are called symptoms. They include making us feel so unwell that we are forced to take to our beds and recharge our batteries through enforced rest; discharging toxins through the skin (rashes, boils, abscesses) or with fevers; clearing the digestive system (nausea, diarrhoea); inflammations to bring healing blood to affected area.

How exactly the body reacts to ill-usage depends on where the weak link is and the stress we put on it. Well-publicized correlations have been those between habitual tension and digestive ulcers, excessive intake of alcohol and liver disorders, smoking and lung cancer, eating too many fatty foods and coronary heart disease, insufficient fibre in the diet and diseases of the colon.

Sometimes we can get a clue from our symptoms as to what is needed to stop putting our systems under so much pressure. If, for example, we are getting spots, skin rashes, boils, going on a cleansing diet of raw foods and juices for a while will co-operate with these efforts being made by our bodies to clean itself up internally. Similarly, with diarrhoea, where the body is trying to throw out rubbish, the indication is in the direction of fasting while drinking plenty of fluids. Disturbed sleep, waking up in the mornings too early could suggest that the body is needing more exercise, raring to go for a jog or to feel itself extended physically in some way. Asthma is often a symptom of anxiety, of being under too much pressure; we are just not giving ourselves breathing space. The language of the body is often just as literal in other ways when it comes to producing symptoms of its 'disease', its distress at what we are doing to it. If we do not get, or allow ourselves to receive, enough support from others, the parts of the body whose job it is to support us could give way under the strain; we can slip a disc or pull a muscle in our leg, suffer low back pain or get varicose veins.

A colleague of mine who is very successful in his field of alternative medicine has been taking on too many commitments recently: too many patients, too many lectures, too many articles It had got to the stage where he hardly had a moment to himself, but his ambition drove him on. He had accepted a gruelling programme which involved leading training groups in several European cities, telling himself this would be the 'holiday' he desperately needed. His body knew better. The night before leaving on his whirlwind tour he was packing. He told me that he was feeling exhausted and he remembered thinking, 'God, I'm tired. How can I do all this?' That very moment he felt a tearing pain in the calf of his right leg. He hardly slept a wink that night with the discomfort of the torn muscle. The next morning it was obvious that he could not travel. The slightest pressure of his foot on the floor was agonizing. He was forced to cancel his commitments for several weeks and rest. Which was, of course, just what he needed. *If we don't take responsibility for our survival, the body will try to do it for us*. At least he didn't suffer a stroke or a heart attack.

Our vital force

A useful way of seeing health and illness is in terms of *energy*. When we talk about 'good resistance' or 'a strong immune system' what we mean is that the body has enough vital force to deal with the threats to it from the environment. Anything that gives us more energy makes us feel more vital, fit, stronger, e.g., sound diet, exercise, sleep and relaxation. Whatever doesn't feed the vital force or drains us, e.g. junk food, stress and any form of excess, makes us feel 'down' and, if our reservoir of energy gets too low, ill. Research in the USSR and recently in the West has shown that it is possible to diagnose certain illnesses even before the symptoms become manifest, by taking photographs of a person's energy field using a process called Kirlian photography. Semyon Kirlian was a Russian electrician who, together with his wife Valentina, discovered how to capture on film the energy field that surrounds each of us, using an aluminium plate to which a high-frequency field is delivered. The energy field (for example, surrounding the subject's hand which had been placed on the plate) came out as colour patterns and whirls. Kirlian found that one day when he was not feeling well the energy field photographed around his hand came out faint and blurred. He compared it with that of Valentina (who was well) only to find that hers was bright and clear.

Strengthening your vital force for immunity, well-being and self-healing

Modern western medicine is, apart from the obvious exception of immunization against mostly tropical diseases like cholera, typhoid and yellow fever, more geared to 'cure' than to prevention of disease. Drugs and surgery are its main weapons and are undoubtedly called for in life-threatening illness. They help the body to cope with invasion or accident by attacking the symptoms, seen as caused by external events. But they do not boost the body's own vital energy which provides the real cure. On the contrary, they deplete it. It has been suggested that AIDS may possibly be a man-made disease, a manifestation on a global scale, not so much of sexual promiscuity, but promiscuity in the abuse of drugs of all kinds that have weakened our natural immune systems.

It has been estimated that every year something in the region of three million unnecessary prescriptions for antibiotics are issued for sore throats. The World Health Organization lists only a few hundred drugs as 'essential'. In Britain we can choose from over six thousand types of antibiotic, and in 1986 a record 397 million prescriptions were dispensed. Antibiotics and surgery are drastic weapons for use only in emergencies. The body then has to recover, not only from the illness, but from the remedy. If we have been hospitalized, this recovery will have to be in spite of food that, for the most part, seems prepared as if there were little connection between diet and health. It behoves us, then, to keep our level of vitality high enough to be out of range of the necessity for such ministrations. The 'Way of Food' is the first line of defence. Here are other ways to strengthen your immune system and to heighten your vitality for well-being and, if you are unwell, to promote healing.

Exercise

Moderate exercise stimulates the immune system, increasing lymphocyte efficiency. It raises the body temperature which in turn stimulates both interferon and the macrophages. Death rates from cancer have been found to be higher among those doing jobs which call for little muscular effort than among those engaged in more strenuous work, while the opportunity afforded by exercise to channel stress may be significant in reducing the incidence of cancer. Certainly the incidence of heart disease has increased in affluent societies, where people eat too much and sit too much.

What exercise you should take, how much and how often, depends on your age, state of health and personal taste. If you have not exercised in years it is advisable to have a medical check-up first and, in any case, to stay within your limits. The benefits of exercise will be enhanced if you choose a form that you enjoy rather than making it a duty. Certainly never before have so many people been concerned with keeping fit and you will not lack for company whether you are jogging and running in the park, swimming at your local pool, working out at the health club gym, or attending your aikido or aerobics class.

If all that sounds too strenuous for you, you could try yoga, which is aimed at raising and harmonizing the vital energy called, in yoga, 'prana'. Unlike the more familiar forms of exercise, yoga works on the glands and nerves, and the spine rather than on muscles. The postures and breathing exercises are designed both to heighten vitality and to relax us – a perfect formula for well-being.

Deep relaxation

Learning how to sink into deep and blissful relaxation at will is to co-operate totally with the body's natural way of recharging its batteries. After all, this is why we go to bed every night, why we take to our beds when we are ill, why doctors order us to rest. If you can switch off totally at the first subtle warnings that all is not well with your body, there is a very good chance that you will not go on to develop overt signs of 'dis-ease'. Freed from outer demands on its energy supply, the body will (if it has not already been too depleted by poor diet, lack of exercise or other abuse) gradually build up its store of energy to safer levels where its immune system is fighting fit again. Deep relaxation also helps to handle pain, which is always made more unbearable by tensing up and by fear. It counteracts the effects of stress, defined by Hans Selye as 'the rate of wear and tear in the human body.'

Relaxing is not something that we do, but what happens when we *stop* doing – and that includes the 'doing' in our heads that we call thinking, planning, calculating, worrying.

Its essence is body awareness, just allowing yourself to experience what is happening from moment to moment in the way of body sensations. Normally, for most of the day, we are more or less unaware of our bodies. Either we are doing, or we are thinking. During either activity our perception of our own bodies is either peripheral or non-existent. To relax deeply we have to (as Fritz Perls put it) 'lose our minds and come to our senses'. Another way of putting it would be that we have to slip out of the left side of our brain over to the right side, from the critical, rational, active function to the feeling, intuitive, passive. The feel of it is of letting go, sinking down opening up.

Practise the following basic relaxation exercise until you get the feel of total relaxation and can 'get there in one', anytime you like. The secret, remember, is: *forget your worries and be in your body.*

Basic relaxation exercise

Ideally this should be done lying down but can be done sitting (as in autogenic training). Make sure you won't be disturbed for at least half an hour. Loosen clothing, take off shoes. The room should be warm enough, lighting subdued. Your head is better unsupported, but you may use a small pillow if that is more comfortable. Arms should be at the sides, palms up or down as you prefer.

Take a few deep, slow breaths, repeating silently the word *relax* as you exhale. Try to imagine yourself out in the open air, in contact with nature somewhere, enjoying the freshness and the freedom of it. You might like to visualize some place you know and love, a beach, perhaps, or a garden, or beautiful countryside where you have walked in the past. Try to see the place in as much detail as you can, or, if visualizing does not come easily to you, try to recapture how it *felt* to lie on this beach, to sit in this garden, to walk along this country lane in the sunshine. Imagine the sounds you would hear. Are they of seagulls wheeling overhead, of birdsong in the trees and hedgerows, of waves lapping the beach or of fountains playing? What are you enjoying most in this idyllic scene?

After enjoying this visualization for a few minutes, let your awareness come into your body, scanning it as though from the inside. What are you in fact aware of right now? Is it:

- your breathing
- the weight of your body on the mattress or the floor
- body sensations, for example, a fatigued muscle, tension around the eyes, the mouth, the belly, an itching foot?

Allow your body to get heavier and heavier, and trust the mattress or floor to support it. Let go of your body as if you wanted to sink through the floor down into the room below. Sense the boundaries of your body. How much space does it take up?

Become aware of your breathing. Don't change it, just feel the rise and fall of your diaphragm as air comes in and goes out again. Scan your body again. Start with the toes in one foot. Feel them one by one – you don't have to wiggle them, just giving them your attention is enough. Slowly let your attention take in the foot. Feel your heel on the floor, the sensitive sole that can be so ticklish, the ankle bone. Still very slowly, become aware of the calf of that leg ... then the knee ... then the shin bone ... then the thigh ... Now feel the weight of the whole leg on the floor, how much heavier it feels than the other, unrelaxed leg.

Start with the toes of the other foot and follow the same sequence. Give yourself as much time as you need. There is no need to rush. Relaxing just one part of the body will help to relax the rest of it. After the legs, become aware of the rest of your body as follows:

- buttocks
- anus
- genitals
- lower back
- spine
- shoulders
- arms (upper arm, elbow, forearm, wrist)
- hands (palm, back of hand, thumb, fingers in turn)
- belly
- neck, head and face (jaws, mouth, eyes).

Just by giving the parts of your body attention in this way will serve to relax and energize them, for body awareness *is* relaxation and attention is energy. If you have the intention to relax from the start of this exercise, you will. Stay in the blissful state of total relaxation for as long as you can, for you are doing your body a whole power of good while you are in this alpha state. It is allowing your body to recoup its energy and to recuperate from the stress it has been subjected to. Do this exercise at least once a day, and whenever you feel stressed or fatigued. It will refresh you as well as a night's sleep would. Above all, do it whenever you feel 'under the weather', or as if you are 'going down with something'. By relaxing deeply in this way, you may not.

Healing visualization

When you are totally relaxed after doing the basic relaxation exercise is the best time to use mental imagery for healing and the relief of pain. Just as you calmed yourself down at the start of the exercise by visualizing yourself enjoying a beautiful and safe place like a beach or a garden, so you can create pictures in your mind that have the power to heal and soothe your body.

The pioneer of the use of visualization, as used currently at the Cancer Help Centres at Bristol and elsewhere, was Dr Carl Simonton, a radiation oncologist and medical director of the Cancer Counselling and Research Centre in Dallas, Texas. Simonton first used visualization in 1971 with a 60-year-old man suffering from advanced throat cancer. The patient was asked to participate in a programme of relaxation and visualization carried out three times a day for five to fifteen minutes, on awakening in the morning, after lunch, and at night before retiring. When he was sufficiently relaxed, he was asked to visualize the cancer cells being attacked by the radiation therapy he was also receiving, in the form of tiny bullets of energy and then to create a picture of his body's white blood cells removing the dead and dying cancer cells. The visualization process finished with seeing the cancer shrinking in size and himself back in blooming health. It worked. The patient gained weight, felt stronger. Two months later he showed no sign of cancer.

The remission of his cancer through his own participation in what was happening to his body put this patient back in charge of his own health. He went on to use the technique to improve his arthritis, smoothing the joint surfaces in his mind to the point where his symptoms had decreased sufficiently for him to enjoy fishing again. Now thoroughly confident, he went on to cure himself of the sexual impotence that had plagued him for twenty years. Using visualizations, he brought his sexual life back to normal within two weeks.

Users of biofeedback have found that trying directly to influence the body's organs and functions is less effective than using imagery. Experiments carried out in 1984 at the George Washington Medical Centre in Washington DC proved that the immune system can be strengthened by visualization. Not only did it increase the amount of white blood cells but also the level of a hormone important to the T helper cells called thymosin-alpha-1. Interestingly enough, this hormone produces a sense of well-being – which suggests once again that the way to *be* well is to get to *feel* well. Visualization is being used today not only in the treatment of cancer but also with AIDS patients, for example, at the Middlesex Hospital in London.

While deeply relaxed, in the alpha state between waking and sleeping, is the best time to practise visualization for healing. Let your attention focus on the part of you that is producing symptoms or pain. Simply by doing this (rather than trying to distract yourself from experiencing it) you will be feeding energy to that part, in the same way as, if you concentrate on a finger, for example, it will start to feel warm because of the increased flow of blood that you are directing to it. Relaxing into pain rather than resisting it banishes the tension and fear that only make it worse. Rather, try to feel love and gratitude to the body that is fighting on your behalf, drawing your attention to the part that is under stress. *Participate in your own healing process by becoming aware of how your body's defences are working on your behalf – and sending it reinforcements in the form of positive mental energy.*

Rather than imposing visualizations, work with whatever images come up as you lie there, feeding attention to the state of the battle going on within your body, staying in the front line rather than deserting in panic. What does your disease look like? Images might be of black blobs, jagged edges, mud or slime, angry red flames or something that seems to have nothing at all to do with anything. Try to work with the image in a way that replaces blackness or darkness, chaos, discord, ugliness, with white or gold light, order, harmony, beauty. You may be a person who finds it easier to feel rather than to visualize. In that case, remember how you used to feel before you were ill and dwell on that feeling of fitness, imagining that you are well and on form again.

Once I had a viral throat infection that made swallowing painful and reduced talking to a hoarse whisper. My doctor declared that antibiotics would do no good and that the infection would just have to run its course. After ten days of using sign language, of feeling I was swallowing razor blades every time I had a cup of tea, of nights disturbed by a ticklish dry cough, I decided it had gone on long enough and that I would try to rid myself of this nuisance by visualization. Focusing my attention on what happened when I swallowed (painfully), the image came up of barbed wire. Staying with the picture, it became a sort of no man's land, like a scene from the trenches in the First World War. It was desolate, muddy, grey, barren, scarred by shell holes. I imagined it as a painting that I could alter any way I wished, using paint-remover and painting over it. Slowly I transformed the scene by painting in blue skies and the sun, carpeting the pitted mud with bright green grass, turning the barbed wire into a hedgerow in full flower. By the time the menacing battlefield had been transformed into a sunlit English meadow I was already feeling better in a subtle way, as if some shadow had lifted, though it still hurt when I swallowed. Next morning on awakening my body felt relaxed even though the throat was still quite sore. Before rising I visualized my meadow again, this time with me sunbathing on the grass. I imagined the warmth of the sun's rays on my body and especially on my throat, soothing it, causing the viruses to shrivel and die. Finally, I conjured up a picture of me conversing with friends, voice back to normal, feeling fit, having a good time again. By the end of that day the voice was husky but the swallowing was no longer painful – and I felt fitter, with more energy than I had had for some time. By the next day everything was back to normal and I had soon forgotten I had ever lost my voice.

We shall be seeing in a later chapter how neurotic and emotional disorders carry their own message if we can decipher them. So, perhaps, do physical symptoms. Often we may be falling ill to avoid situations or decisions, to allow ourselves to be cared for, or as a cry for help. Making patients aware of their unconscious wish to be ill was an important part of Simonton's work, as well as visualization.

Staying positive

Hans Selye was the pioneer of the modern concept of stress. In his book *The Stress of Life* he drew attention to the effects of negative emotions on the chemistry of the body, how frustration or unexpressed anger could cause adrenal exhaustion. Research in the new area of study called psychoneuroimmunology is confirming that attitudes can kill or cure. Just as positive visualizations can cause remission of cancer, so negative feelings can cause it. Our hormones are affected by our feelings. They are transmitted from the limbic system to the hypothalamus, a part of the brain that controls output of hormones via the pituitary gland. Stressful feelings (for example, anger, fear, depression) release a powerful immuno-suppressant called cortisol. Cortisol reduces the number of T-cells and interferon, and increases T-suppressors. At Harvard Medical School a research team found that higher immune activity went with positive attitudes, impaired immune activity with negative ones. Norman Cousins in his bestseller *Anatomy of an Illness* describes how he cured himself of ankylosing spondylitis, a painful, crippling and untreatable disease – by laughter and high doses of vitamin C. It was when he decided that his massive prescribed doses of painkillers (26 aspirin tablets and 12 phenylbutazone a day) were doing him no good and sent out for *Candid Camera* videos and old Marx Brothers films instead that he started on the road to recovery from what he had been told was an incurable disease.

Another survivor through participating positively in his illness has been the American, Louis Nassaney. Diagnosed with Kaposi's Sarcoma (KS) in May 1983, for seven months he played the role of an 'AIDS victim', spending most of his time in bed at his parents' home. Inspired by the support of his father, however, he decided to drop the victim role and fight to get well again. His doctors were suggesting chemotherapy, since gamma interferon treatment was having no effect. Instead he chose a programme of vitamin therapy, exercise, acupuncture, visualization, affirmations, deep relaxation and meditation. He gives much credit to his 'metaphysical counsellor', Louise Hay, for what followed. She taught him to visualize the KS lesion on his thigh as a pencil mark. Every night he would create a mental image of himself erasing the lesion with a pencil rubber. He also visualized his helper cells as rabbits, reproducing themselves at a tremendous rate. After four months the lesion began to fade and, in October 1984, a biopsy at the Los Angeles Hospital where he had been treated, revealed only dead scar tissue. He has been well ever since and is described as being in 'complete remission'. That he can't be doing too badly is proved by the fact that he came fourth out of fifty contestants in a 'Mr Superman' physique contest at the Hollywood Palladium! He is currently touring the USA spreading a message of hope for other 'AIDS victims'. The core of his message is: 'No one will heal physically if they don't love themselves first.'

His story and those of other AIDS survivors now beginning to be reported from the United States, should do much to encourage, not only those diagnosed as HIV positive, but anyone casting themselves in the role of victim of whatever 'disease', to bring some positive energy to their situation and to work to strengthen their immune system and vital force. Rather than feeding the mind with the paranoia of the press, with labels like 'incurable' and 'invariably fatal', nourish and empower the part of you that has the power to heal you, God willing, with positive affirmations. Here are a few you could try.

- *Every day, in every way, I'm getting better and better*

- *I deserve to enjoy radiant health*
- *Every day I feel stronger and more alive*
- *I love myself totally and am allowing my body to heal itself*
- *I no longer need to be ill. I have learned what I needed to learn*
- *I relax into my body and trust all is happening as it should*
- *I love life and want more of it.*

Make up your own, specifically geared to your condition and repeat them with faith that they will make you feel better. Affirmations, like the visualizations to accompany them, are made most effectively during moments of total relaxation.

It cannot be emphasized enough that taking charge of our health in the ways described above is not *instead of* seeking medical aid but *as well as*. It is time we stopped talking of 'alternative therapies' and spoke rather of 'complementary therapies'. The healing arts of the future must come to embrace all that has been proved to work – even if we may not be sure why it works, as for example in the case of homoeopathic remedies. That this is, in fact, beginning to happen is evidenced by the growing number of medical doctors who are training in homoeopathy and acupuncture and by the establishment of the Cancer Help Centres. The model for future National Health Centres may well be the St Marylebone Healing and Counselling Centre in London where doctors, counsellors, priests, healers, music therapists, acupuncturists and osteopaths work side by side.

Health care statistics become more frightening, both numerically and financially: 7.6 million hospitalized in one year; a waiting list of nearly 700,000; the taxpayers footing a £23 billion bill this year; 24 million prescriptions for drugs like Librium, Valium and Mogadon written out each year; tens of thousands of old people addicted to tranquillizers . . . From every point of view it would definitely seem to be time for each and every one of us to start taking charge of our own health.

CHAPTER 7

Switching off the pressure

But wherefore do not you a mightier way
Make war upon this bloody tyrant Time?

Sonnet 16

Do you feel . . .

under pressure
tense, unable to unwind
at everyone's beck and call
burdened with too many commitments
that you never have any time for yourself
always in a rush to keep up with what has to be done
resenting all the work you have to do
worrying about the future
at a loss when you have nothing to do
guilty when you take it easy
unable sometimes to sleep for the thoughts rushing
round in your head?

In the last chapter we suggested that practising the basic
relaxation exercise daily would help to repair the wear and
tear on our nerves and bodies that we call stress. But unless
we change our life-styles as well, it is rather like trying to fill a
bucket with holes in it. The energy built up by going down to
the alpha state will be dissipated quickly again if we are taking
on more than we can handle in the way of commitments and
rushing ourselves into an early grave.

It is estimated that one in every three men suffers a heart
attack in the course of his working life. Stress contributes
much to the death toll from the biggest single killer in the

western world today. But knowing how to handle the stress that is part and parcel of modern living is essential, not only to avoid having a coronary, but also for enjoying quality in our lives. *We feel oppressed when we don't give ourselves enough time and space.*

Victims of time are probably the commonest types of victim around today. In one sense, of course, the whole human race is at the mercy of the 'tyrant' Time. It does not consult us as to the most convenient moment for us to be born or to die. It makes these appointments for us and we keep them willy-nilly. It is kinder to some than to others, but, gracefully or not, we all get older. What it gives with one hand it takes with the other. In return for longevity we have to put up with ailing bodies and with watching our loved ones die before us. We regret the past, agonize over the future. Yet still,

The Moving Finger writes; and, having writ,
Moves on: nor all thy Piety nor Wit
Shall lure it back to cancel half a Line
Nor all thy Tears wash out a Word of it.

Rubaiyat of Omar Khayyam
(l.71)

Time is a bitch, and the bitch goddess has never been so worshipped as today. We are brought up to believe that 'wasting' time is akin to sin, that 'the Devil makes work for idle hands'. 'Saving' time is seen nowadays as a value in itself, and as a result of so many advertising slogans, associated with efficiency. Speed sells: 'lightning' cleaners, 'whirlwind' floor mops, 'fast' food, 'instant' coffee . . .

But pace has its price. Our modern culture that developed jet travel and labour-saving gadgets is also killing itself or going mad with the stress it generates. The faster we go, the harder we fall. Add to that too much pace, not enough space: overcrowded cities, traffic congestion, noise and other sensory over-stimulation, and, compounding our sense of oppression, the conditioning that makes it selfish or unsociable to take space for ourselves. It is not surprising that after a day working in inner cities, commuters look deadbeat, strap-hanging in packed rush-hour trains, drained and lifeless, for all the world like corpses on a gibbet. *Make more*

time, take more space for yourself.
Here are some changes you could try making.

Set boundaries

Don't complain that other people invade your space and make demands on your time if you have not made it clear to them what you are prepared to give and to accept. A homoeo-path I know is plagued by patients' phone calls during the evening (and sometimes late at night). They ring to tell him the remedy he gave them is or is not working, ask what to make of new symptoms, etc. He is fed up with this invasion of his privacy but cannot bring himself to say anything because he thinks he should be available to them whenever they need him. If we do not set our own boundaries we risk getting landed with those set by others. As we suggested in an earlier chapter, 'burn-out' is a hazard of the helping professions if the helper doesn't know when to stop feeding others and give some time to feeding himself or herself.

If we ourselves do not set clear boundaries we get landed with others'. Sometimes merely putting an imaginary ring around oneself is effective in drawing back in one's energy when one has been giving out too much. This can be useful in crowded, noisy places when you are starting to feel drained. Parents particularly can avoid being driven to distraction by demanding children by setting clear boundaries as to what is acceptable behaviour and what isn't. If they are consistent, and the boundaries are appropriate to the child's state of development, their effect will be positive. The child will feel more held, secure, and learn how to tolerate the frustration of his omnipotence that will be forthcoming in later life.

Cut down on your commitments

Don't overstructure your time, whether through greed or anxiety, for example, not wanting to miss out, fear that you might be left with emptiness, with nothing happening at all, of having to say 'no'. Give yourself time to think what taking in any more commitments will entail before you agree to adding to your burdens. You might have to look at your priorities. How much is extra leisure worth to you? Do you really need the extra pay from overtime or accepting another job? How important is it not to risk offending somebody else by turning them down? What comes first, your health and quality of life, or money and popularity?

Slow down

Ask yourself 'Why am I rushing right now?' You might be late for that appointment, but so what? What do you fear might happen if you are late? Take responsibility for not allowing yourself enough time. If there really wasn't enough time, how come you agreed to meet this appointment in the first place? If you are delayed because of some reason beyond your control, then what's the problem? They will just have to accept your reason for being late, that's all. Let other people do some work in looking at their own expectations of you. Remember, you are not their mother (nor are they yours!). And, if you rush yourself into a coronary, it will be yours and not theirs. Do yourself a favour and take your time. Nothing is that important.

Follow your own rhythm

There is a time for working and a time for rest, a time for being with others and a time for being in your own space. If you are not going so fast that you have lost touch with your own inner needs you will sense it. It is when we lose touch with our own process that we feel persecuted and blame others for 'making' us work too much, for draining us of energy. But it is always our own responsibility to withdraw from situations when we have had enough. Nobody ever *gives* us space. We have to ask for it – or simply *take* it. It doesn't have to be done in a heavy way. Just to say that you need some space right now should be enough – and then withdraw. If it's not enough and you get a negative reaction, then your inclination to withdraw is probably right – they are probably draining you by wanting your attention or having expec-

tations of you, otherwise they would understand and allow
you to do what you have said you need to do.

Be with yourself more

Either enjoy being in others' company or choose to enjoy
your own company. What we sometimes find ourselves doing
is dithering somewhere in the middle, uncomfortable with
being just one of a crowd or losing our individuality in a
group, and fearful of being alone. We suggested in an earlier
chapter that the 'bottom line' with all of us, a hangover from
early childhood, is this dread of being abandoned and being
left totally alone. It is a barrier to empowerment to be overcome, for it is in our moments of aloneness with ourselves
(not at all the same as loneliness, absence of the other) that
bliss can be experienced. The pressure of others' expectations is off, we relax into ourselves, recharge our batteries,
have the time to reflect on our lives, where we are now and
where we are going, and get inspiration and support from
our subconscious.

The fact that many more people are practising yoga,
meditation, t'ai-chi, aikido and other martial arts, traditional
eastern techniques for slowing down, centring and tuning in
to one's own process and energy, suggests that these deeper
needs are not being encouraged or catered for in our own
culture. Whether or not we choose to go along to classes and
learn the form, we would certainly benefit from trying to
apply in daily life and work the principles on which they are
all based, namely:

- *present-centredness*
- *one-pointedness*
- *effortlessness.*

These are about trying to be more aware of what we are doing
at any moment, of what is happening around us but remaining centred in ourselves while we are doing so. They are
about learning to give our total attention to the task in hand
but in a relaxed way, without strain or effort. They are, above
all, about freeing ourselves from the domination of our minds

that cloud the vividness of our experience of the present moment. They prevent us from really feeling the present, by making us *think* about it, or, taking us right away from it, fantasizing about the past or the future. Mind and Time are twin tyrants oppressing us all. *Being here now, being present as totally as we can, frees us from both.*

Practise daily meditation

Did you react to this suggestion with, 'What, me – meditate?' You may have the idea of meditation as something exotically oriental and may be recoiling from the idea of your bedroom smelling of incense all night. But, in fact, meditation is not just for orientals; it can help all of us relax back into ourselves when we come home from the pressure of being out in the world and, often, out of ourselves. It is true that meditation was developed in the East but then, why should we not learn from them the way to inner tranquillity as Japan, for example, has learned (perhaps too well) from the West the way to technological supremacy? And we are indeed learning already, for example in our concern for conservation, to respect and value life in all its forms and to work in harmony with Mother Nature, a concept that would have been very familiar to a Taoist in ancient China, or would be today to a Buddhist in South-East Asia. The fact that one can get acupuncture on the National Health is an indication of the increasing respectability in the West of traditional Eastern methods of healing. It has been proved by scientific tests that meditating is good for you, acting as an antidote against the bad effects of the pace and pressures of modern living. It

- decreases the activity of the sympathetic nervous system activated in fight/flight responses
- decreases blood lactate, a substance produced by the metabolism of skeletal muscles and associated with anxiety states
- decreases the heart-rate and respiration, with calming effect
- induces alpha brainwaves associated with deeply relaxed states.

There are other ways of slowing down and counteracting the effects of stress (for example, autogenics) and these are explored in my book *How To Beat Fatigue* (Century Arrow 1986).

Here, though, are three simple meditation techniques you could try out (on different occasions, not in the same session) to see if meditation is for you, and if it is, which technique feels most natural to you. The aim of all meditation techniques is the same – to slow down our thought process, to bring us out of our heads back into awareness of what is happening in and around us, and just allowing ourselves to experience that *as it is*, not trying to change it in any way, accepting, passive but alert, a watcher.

The best times to meditate are on an empty stomach, early morning or early evening, though a cup of tea won't do any harm beforehand – in fact it might help to make you more alert. Try to meditate always in the same room and it helps if the room is a quiet one in which you can relax. Arrange not to be disturbed for however long you want to meditate: fifteen to twenty minutes will probably be enough to begin with.

Sit, either on a chair (feet on the floor), or on a cushion (tailor fashion), or kneel (buttocks resting on heels) – it doesn't matter so long as you are comfortable enough to hold the same position without fidgeting, which would be distracting. Whichever position you choose, keep your back straight without straining. Eyes may be either closed or half-open, gaze resting on a point on the floor in front of you that feels right, but soft and unfocused. Your left hand should be resting lightly, palm upward, in the right hand with the tips of both thumbs gently touching.

Meditation on the breath

Breathe normally, but become aware of it. Let your attention be on the tip of the nose and feel the incoming and outgoing breaths on your nostrils. After each outgoing breath, in the pause before you breathe in again, count silently: 'one' (breathe in/breathe out), 'two' (breathe in/breathe out), 'three', and so on up to ten – then start again from 'one'. If you lose the sequence, start again at 'one'. Your mind will try to distract you from giving your total attention to counting the breaths. Pay no attention to it. You don't *need* to think about anything right now – you are in fact meditating precisely in order to relax from having to think at all!

Listening meditation

Just that. Be very passive, just hearing any sounds that want to be heard. Don't discriminate between pleasant sounds and harsh sounds. Listen to the sounds of traffic, for example, passing cars, motorcycles, police or ambulance sirens, as if you were listening to the different instruments in an orchestra. Just being aware of what is, and letting it be there, is what meditation is all about.

Witnessing meditation

What are you aware of at this very moment? Allow yourself to experience whatever comes into your awareness from moment to moment. Don't try to impose anything, don't choose 'this' rather than 'that'. Let whatever comes, come, however trivial. You might become conscious of things outside you (for example, sounds, or threads on the carpet in front of you), or things inside you (for example, feeling bored, or an itchy foot). Be totally impartial. It doesn't matter what you are aware of, that is not the point. The point is to be in the present. Meditating is being here now.

But perhaps you are meditating already without knowing it, for example when you swim or jog on your own, are absorbed in listening to music or playing an instrument, walking in the countryside soaking up the beauty of nature around you, or perhaps enjoying a long soak in the bath.

Sitting meditations like the ones described above are not the only forms of meditation. Anything can become a meditation so long as you really experience whatever activity you happen to be engaged in, while remaining aware of who is doing it, that is, you. This is what Gurdjieff called 'self-remembering', and is behind the Buddhist practice of reminding yourself regularly during the day of what it is you are engaged in at this moment.

For example, when things at the office are getting on top of you and you are feeling under pressure, victimized by the work or the boss, come back into your own centre by reminding yourself who you are, where you are, what you are doing ('typing, typing' or, perhaps, 'fuming, fuming'!). It might be a good idea to remind yourself also why you are doing it at all ('money, money'?) to get back in touch with having chosen to put yourself in that office in the first place. Reminding ourselves when we feel oppressed by something that *we* chose to create oppression in our lives dispels the illusion of 'poor me, victim', and creates a whole new reality for ourselves. We take charge of our time and what happens in our space when we choose to fill it with things to enjoy (as, of course, we do in our leisure hours). 'That holiday feeling' is the exact opposite of the victim state and is the state of consciousness to aim for even when we may not actually be on holiday. When we find ourselves repeating to ourselves 'enjoying, enjoying' *whatever* we are doing, we are out of the time and space trap.

CHAPTER 8

How to be your own counsellor

Be to yourself
As you would to your friend

King Henry VIII (I.i)

Do you . . .

lack confidence
often feel depressed
have a low opinion of yourself
wish you could be a better person
blame yourself a lot
hate yourself for feeling the way you do
compare yourself unfavourably with others
feel horribly insecure sometimes
fear meeting new people
try hard to cover up how vulnerable you feel
feel guilty a lot of the time
find it hard to express yourself
continually judge yourself
feel isolated
think you're abnormal
feel cut off from your feelings
have trouble handling your anger or jealousy
feel unsupported?

If so, you are like many people who eventually get so fed up with feeling bad about themselves that they seek counselling.

In this chapter are outlined ways in which you can help yourself to handle your emotions, to feel more confident and at ease with yourself by treating yourself the way a professional counsellor would. This is in fact what happens if counselling has been successful. The client introjects the counsellor, learns gradually to replace his or her own harsh and punitive 'shoulds' with the acceptance, the 'unconditional positive regard' shown by the counsellor. In other words, to see himself or herself with more loving eyes, with more understanding and less judgement.

It is probably true to say that none of us, if we are truly honest, feels deep down that they are 'good enough'. How exactly may or may not be clear to us: we may feel inadequate generally, or only in a specific area. This sense of 'not measuring up' may be strong or dimly felt, may follow us like a shadow all the time or only on a bad day. Alfred Adler built his whole approach to psychotherapy on this universal inferiority complex and saw much of what human beings do as attempts to compensate for the unpleasant feeling of insecurity it arouses within them. We may deny it, pretend to be God's gift to women, the belle of the ball, the cat's whiskers. We may 'give ourselves airs', especially an air of confidence, though the truth might well be that we have to steel ourselves to meet new people, whether in the course of our work or at a party. We all learn the tricks that hide our vulnerability. We don't want anyone to see it because we can't bear to see it ourselves. *You are not the only one who is trying to hide how vulnerable you are. Others perhaps are doing it with less awareness than you.*

They are the power-seekers and manipulators of this world, the ones who are driven by ambition and the need to control others. Unaware of their emotional insecurity, it drives and controls *them*. You, at least, are in touch with your feelings of insecurity – which gives you a head start. Now you need to be more aware of how you let them control you.

We use props as protection, small talk as a means of flight from present reality, to fill uncomfortable silences; rationality to suppress threatening feelings; sexuality to avoid emotional intimacy that would *really* strip us naked. Too tense and insecure to just relax and play, we play roles instead: macho man, perhaps, or seductress to hide our fear that we may not be lovable just for who we are. We hide behind our masks like the actors in ancient Greece, playing the roles that please our audience, that they expect of us. Afraid to show who we are, we try to be what we are not. Eventually we may forget who we are and become indentified with our roles. Ask someone, 'Who are you?' and, more likely than not, the reply will be what they do for a living. *Taking charge of your life is about playing roles but not identifying with them.*

Jung called this recovering our authenticity from the false self behind which is hidden the process of 'individuation'. It takes courage to learn to be our true selves, for we have to confront the vulnerability that made us need our masks in the first place, that made us deny our true feelings because we got the message that they were unacceptable, would make us unlovable. Daring to acknowledge what you are really feeling to yourself, however much you would rather not feel this way, is the way to start counteracting this conditioning, to start giving yourself permission to be who you really are at this moment. *Accepting yourself, not trying to change yourself, is the goal of psychotherapy.* Warts and all. And that means accepting not only the 'nice' parts of yourself but also, in fact, especially, the not-so-nice parts that we all have. Don't try to be 'good', try to be human. Aim at wholeness, not 'perfection'. Otherwise you could go mad.

Respect your feelings, especially the negative ones

We saw in an earlier chapter how repressing feelings, especially negative ones, could damage your health. Our emotional states affect our bodies: our hearts beat faster, there is an increase of blood pressure, adrenal activity, production of corticoids, and flow of hydrochloric acid to the stomach. We flush with anger, blush with embarrassment. Fear drains our cheeks, contracts our stomachs, tenses our muscles. Repression of negative feelings has been linked with a whole range of dis-eases. The medical press is increasingly drawing attention to the dangerous effects of undischarged negative emotions. Grief, shock and anger are now being linked with cancer, for example. The energy has to go somewhere. If it is not consciously acknowledged, expressed and integrated, it could turn malignant and run amok inside us.

Remember that to acknowledge a feeling doesn't mean you have to act it out. Allowing yourself to experience grief doesn't mean that your fear of being swamped by it will lead to breakdown. You are more likely to break down if you *don't* go through the stages of mourning that include numbness, grief, anger at being abandoned, guilt, regret. Admitting to yourself that you are feeling murderous doesn't mean that you have to go out and kill somebody. In fact, you are less likely to do so if you acknowledge to yourself that you are really angry – and then look into why this is so. If you deny and repress the anger it will still be there like an abscess, festering in the subconscious, seeping bitterness, sarcasm, discontent. Resentment can accumulate into a sense of grievance that could indeed lead to violent confrontation. Or it could kill *you*.

It is understandable that we are afraid to acknowledge, let alone allow ourselves to feel, negative emotions. We fear losing control, being swamped by them, being destructive, that we will be stuck with them for ever if we allow them in. They threaten our image of ourselves: we don't like to see ourselves as mean, bitchy, envious, greedy, and all the other things we have been taught are 'not nice'. Nor do we want others to see these sides of us. They might go away, abandon us.

Much that is healing in psychotherapy and counselling is the discovery by clients that daring to acknowledge these darker aspects of themselves (Jung's 'shadow') is not as catastrophic as they feared. The therapist is neither shocked nor disgusted – and continues to treat them with the same 'unconditional positive regard' as before. It is a relief for the clients to realize that they can express anger without the parent figure, represented by the therapist, being either destroyed by it or abandoning them. On the contrary, they will work together to try to understand the hurt behind the anger or the need behind the greed. In the process the meaning of the emotions becomes clear: they are as much signals of the psyche's distress as physical symptoms are of the body's. Not to heed either is dangerous for both our mental and physical health. *Don't suppress your feelings. Look into them and learn from them about who you really are and what you need to be happy.*

Treat yourself as a counsellor would treat you. Be patient with yourself in all your moods, respect your emotions *whatever they may be.* Don't deny. Don't be afraid of them. They are not demonic, neither are you omnipotent. Allowing them to be there may be uncomfortable, even painful, but at least you will know where they are and that you are processing them out of your system, not absorbing their energy into the fibres of your body. In my book *Coming Alive* (Thorsons 1987), you will find techniques used in therapy for harmlessly discharging negative energy without hurting anyone, including yourself. Here is the basic technique for handling any highly-charged negative emotions that threaten to swamp you.

Catharsis

Let off some of the steam in a way that you will not regret later after you have calmed down again. You could get some relief by:

- directly confronting the object of your wrath – after all, they may have treated you badly and deserve a telling-off or to hear some home truths
- if this is too risky or inappropriate, if, for example, the feelings are of grief, sharing with a sympathetic listener helps (anyone you feel held and heard by, who is able to really *listen* will do)
- going out for a run, a jog or a walk to help disperse some of the energy.

Dancing (though you may not feel like it) is also good. Taking deep breaths and giving your body a good shake makes you feel better. Give yourself permission to cry like a baby – it will cleanse you. Anger, too, when it is clean and a real response in the moment, may not only be totally appropriate, it can be beautiful. Remember the way Jesus went for the money-lenders in the temple? At least you, and those around you, will know you are alive – and can roar when you need to!

Staying in the present
This will stop you fuelling the negative energy by dredging up
the past or getting into a panic about the future. It will also
give you a sense of being in control, as if you were watching
your feelings from a distance.

- Be aware of your body sensations – what you are
  actually experiencing *in your body* now that you are
  'angry' or 'depressed' or 'jealous'?
- Be aware of your surroundings, who you are and where
  you are. This will ground you and, if you need to act on
  your feelings, will enable you to do so more appropriately and effectively.

If you do not resist your feelings and emotions, if you
acknowledge and accept them, they will pass and leave you in
peace. *What we resist, persists*. We shall be seeing in the next
chapter how we can learn much that is of value about ourselves from our negativity if, after we have calmed down, we
try to bring some insight into *why* we got so upset, *how* our
needs are not being met. Personal growth is very much about
bringing the light of awareness to the disowned shadow side
of ourselves. There, among the discarded rubbish, we often
discover discarded gems. Here are some other ways you can
bring the counsellor's 'unconditional positive regard' into the
way you handle your emotions.

Learn to love your neurosis

There is no way you will get rid of it otherwise. We will never
succeed in changing anything we don't like in ourselves by
resisting it on the level of the ego, that is, consciously. Telling
yourself it shouldn't be there, hating yourself for it, hoping it
will go away, changes nothing. It won't, because your unconscious has put it there for a purpose. *The purpose of our
neurotic symptoms is to protect us, either from attack from
without, or from breakdown*. Not only this, but, according to
Jung, they point the way in the direction of integration and
individuation. Like our bodies, our psyches are self-regulating,
always trying to keep us in balance, to correct the one-
sidedness of our conscious attitudes. However much you

hate what you term 'neurotic' in yourself, be grateful to it for it has helped you to survive so far. If you had not developed it, for example, as a barrier against situations or feelings you couldn't handle, you might have found these too stressful and become schizophrenic. Take responsibility for choosing at some level to defend yourself in this way. Look into the meaning and purpose of this 'neurotic' part of you. How does it protect you? Why did you need to put it there in the first place? A basic rule of psychotherapy to remember: *never attack defences directly – seek to understand their purpose.*

Regain control of the mechanism that you are allowing to control you simply because you have not brought it into consciousness. *Whatever we remain unconscious of controls us.* Ride the horse the way it is going, don't resist and be dragged along. For example, if you suffer from agoraphobia, *choose* not to go out – and get in touch with how this in some way saves you from something else. If you are sexually impotent, *decide* not to have sex – and become aware of how this may actually be more in line with either what you really want or what you need. If you stammer, tune into perhaps why you don't really *want* to speak at all, what is the fear. You abandon the victim role and take charge as soon as you take responsibility, if only by saying to yourself,'one part of me wants to do this, another part of me doesn't'. You may be absolutely right in saying 'no', given your perception of the situation. Get to know how you are trying to protect yourself and against what. Test the reality and the nature of the threat. Perhaps what was perceived as threatening when you were very small, you could take in your stride now that you are fully grown. Take a few small risks, experimenting with relaxing your defences when you feel safe enough to do so. This is the behavioural approach which has proved the most successful (perhaps the only successful) therapy for dealing with phobias. Perhaps your defences may never, in fact, be needed. Keep them in reserve, though – just in case!

Respect your boundaries

A basic concept in Gestalt therapy is that of the *contact*

boundary. This decides how much intimacy we can tolerate with others. If we are unaware of it or do not respect it we will put ourselves in situations where we feel uncomfortable or under stress. For example, we may stay in contact longer than we should, and then wonder why we feel inadequate, with nothing to say, or false, because we are talking when we really don't feel like it. If, therefore, you reproach yourself for being withdrawn, not the life and soul of the party, too shy, wish you were more extroverted, you need to take responsibility for staying within your own space more, for being more sensitive to when you feel confident or safe enough to reach out beyond your boundaries to make contact with others, and when you don't. *Don't compare your boundaries with other people's*. What might be fun for them may be stressful for you. A party that's becoming a 'rave-up' for some may be turning into a nightmare for others more sensitive. What you may enjoy as 'horseplay' may feel aggressive and threatening to me. *It is up to us to withdraw when we've had enough.*

Peter has just terminated counselling after forty sessions. His presenting problem when he first came was his feeling of inadequacy and isolation. He felt tongue-tied when he was with others, never knew what to say when they tried to get to know him. Since they got nothing back from him for their attempts at conversation they would eventually give up. He was living like a hermit apart from the minimal contact he had with colleagues at work in the course of his job as a filing clerk.

As long as he kept making efforts to be less withdrawn nothing happened, except that he felt even more uptight and inadequate. Sooner or later the rather desperate attempts to make conversation dried up and he was left feeling more gauche and isolated than before. Things started to change for him when I encouraged him to become aware of his contact boundary and, within the safety of the therapeutic structure we had created together, Peter started to experiment with staying within his limits or going outside them. Session after session I would ask him to set the boundary between us where *he* wanted it to be, where he felt most comfortable. He would share what he was experiencing as he did so, on a sliding scale between 'safe' and 'scary', 'comfortable' and 'exposed'.

As well as monitoring his own anxiety level and playing with establishing closeness or distance between us, Peter would share the memories and associations that came up.

What emerged was a story of maternal over-protection. He had been a rather sickly child and his anxious mother had virtually suffocated him with her attentions, leaving him no space or allowing him to do anything for himself. He got in touch with feeling hemmed in, with a sense of impotence to do anything for himself. He began to realize that what he had been fighting, his tendency to withdraw, was in fact an expression of his need to get some space for himself. He had never been able to ask for it directly, either his mother would not have heard or she would have been hurt – and he would have felt guilty. He had not learned how to be with another person and not lose his centre. Peter feared everybody who tried to get close to him as another space invader like his mother. His withdrawal served the purpose of retaining some sense of who he was, saved him feeling that he was disappearing into the other, without having to take the responsibility for rejecting their overtures. He eventually formulated the statement behind his failure to respond socially: 'I want you to give me more space. Leave me alone. I need to know I can do things by myself.'

What therapy did for him was to make conscious the unconscious complex that was controlling him. He now had a choice, and, with awareness of his needs for autonomy and how his contact boundary worked, could exercise it. The experience in the counselling room of staying in silence with another person for often extended periods and not being rejected, of being given lots of space to initiate when he felt like it, of relating to somebody he trusted who was not trying to control him, were what he needed to put him back in charge of his own process. Now when he's talking he's talking; when he's not, he's not. But he doesn't make it a problem.

Don't label yourself

What needs to be changed is not who we are but how we see ourselves. We saw in an earlier chapter how anything can be seen in either a positive or a negative light. It depends on what the observer brings to the observed in the way of values, past experience, expectations and so on. Traits that I might find endearing in a person may be driving you round the bend. We can think of Mrs Thatcher as a strong and effective leader or an uncaring Iron Lady; of Prince Charles as extra-ordinarily aware and tuned in – or somewhat eccentric.

Judgements say more about us than about those we judge. They are who they are, the labels are ours. Beware of the labels you stick on yourself (or anyone else tries to) or you will be stuck with them. You will start believing that this is you, start limiting yourself to behaving only in accordance with them. I can think of few more horrific things than feeling expected to react in the same way for the rest of my life, be it 'extroverted' or 'introverted', 'sensitive' or 'thick-skinned', 'jolly' or 'quiet'. Much of what a therapist does is to help you peel off these labels that have become strait-jackets, allowing you to break free of the rigidity of seeing things from only one angle, usually a negative one.

Just as one can judge a room as 'lived in', or 'a pigsty', a scent as 'fragrant' or 'smelly', so what one does or how one is can equally be judged flatteringly or harshly. *De gustibus non est disputandum.* The verdict is entirely subjective. The difference, though, is between feeling good about yourself or feeling miserable. So how have you been labelling yourself? Positively or negatively, affectionately or harshly?

Do you label yourself

well-built or fat	diplomatic or phoney
slim or skinny	sociable or intrusive
high-energy or hyperactive	sensitive or soft
quiet or boring	strong or bossy
down-to-earth or vulgar	sensible with money or
lively or loud	mean
dependable or predictable	vulnerable or cowardly
concerned or nosey	shrewd or calculating?

Joyce certainly has a fuller and more satisfying life now that she has stopped labelling herself. Hers was 'spinster – on the shelf'. True to her label she was playing out the part to perfection. She dressed frumpily, avoided relating to her male colleagues in the publishing house where she worked in any but a sisterly or motherly way. She had women friends she had known for years, but came to counselling because she was becoming aware that she felt dominated by them, was always giving in to where they wanted to go, what they wanted to do. Joyce would never compete with other women for the attention to men. She felt she just wouldn't stand a chance. She complained that she felt patronized by her friends. It turned out that in fact she felt patronized by everybody, including the boss and the other men in the office.

We worked with her self-image which, as is nearly always the case, was poor. It turned out that she was angry at not being seen as interesting in her own right, that she was never invited out to dinner, that others had relationships and she didn't, etc., etc. She blamed her loneliness and frustration on her age (she is in her early forties) and the fact that she was unmarried. 'You have to be in a couple to get invited, otherwise people feel awkward,' she said. We tested the reality of her notion that she was some sort of freak because she had never married, her assumption that 'out there', Everywoman was living happily ever after with Mr Right and that, in the breaks from ecstatic coupling, they would get to feeling sorry for 'poor Joyce who doesn't have what we have'. In reality, the only couple she knew who seemed to be getting on well were her sister and her husband. Every other couple she knew were either 'always having dramas', on the verge of splitting up, or staying together for the sake of the children.

We explored her fantasies about how her life would be different if she were married or in a relationship. Somewhat to her own surprise, she found herself talking about loss of independence, having to 'put up with' having another person around when you wanted to be on your own, having to give up the flat she loved because it would be too small for two, being 'tied down', not being free to go where she wanted when she wanted. She started to get in touch with the 'free spirit' in her that loved her own company, was imaginative, adventurous, and something of a bohemian, the parts of her that made her 'interesting' and alive and had not been allowed expression because of her identification with being a maiden aunt. She began to see herself now, not as a reject, 'on the shelf', but unattached, independent and fancy-free. Her model was now that of a modern career woman who was without a relationship because she had set it up that way. *When you choose what you get you are back in charge.* Now that she values herself more she takes more pride in her appearance and the way she dresses, and is beginning to experience her body as not unattractive. She recounted triumphantly how, when a bitchy friend had tried to put her down at a party with a 'mutton dressed as lamb' comment she was not prepared for Joyce's immediate response to this negativity, a resounding self-validation ending with a request 'not to give me that shit anymore'. And she doesn't get that shit anymore.

Stop putting yourself down

Never allow anyone to invalidate you, and that includes you. *If you don't value who you are, don't expect others to.*

We are usually far harsher on ourselves than on others. Often, if we were to treat them the way we treat ourselves we would be accused of sadism. If you are continually undermining your confidence by self-criticism it's no wonder you don't have any. We are not in this world to be perfect, but to be human. Anyway, what do you want to be perfect *for*? And who are you comparing yourself with? Everybody else is perfectly imperfect too, so, unless you want to be special, drop any ideas of perfection – you'll drive yourself mad. Catch yourself out trying to be perfect by becoming more aware of how you talk to yourself in your head and what you are telling yourself. Would you put up with someone on your back all the time telling you off? That's exactly what you may be doing. Here's how to get off your own back – and how to get your confidence back.

Whenever you catch yourself thinking or saying something

negative about yourself, cancel it out immediately by formulating a positive statement about yourself that contradicts it. Remember,

> There is nothing either good or bad,
> but thinking makes it so.

So you may as well stop giving yourself a bad time. Unless of course, you want to, in which case you are not a victim but a masochist, which is OK. You know what you are doing, you're in charge. If, on the other hand, you don't enjoy feeling bad about yourself, change it by using affirmations. These have been shown to be powerful enough to produce desired responses in the body (for example, in autogenic training for relaxation and self-healing). If they can do this they certainly can affect the subtler mind-energies we call thoughts to improve self-image and banish depressive thinking. Here are some you could try out for a start before working out your own.

Examples of positive affirmations

Every day, in every way, I'm getting better and better

I feel good about myself

I feel more and more confident every day

I love myself just as I am

I am totally lovable for being just the way I am

I am free to be any way I want to be

It's OK for me to feel this way

I give myself permission to feel ... (angry, vicious, mean, jealous, etc.)

This is what I do – and that's OK

This, too, shall pass

I forgive myself for making that mistake

I am here to be human, not perfect

I feel vulnerable – and that's OK.

They should always be framed as a positive, not a negative, statement, for example, 'I enjoy meeting people' instead of 'I am not afraid of people'. Repeat the affirmation several times, each time accentuating a different word. Say it as if you mean it. What you are in fact doing is exercising a new choice to replace one you made that is not in your interests anymore. That is your freedom. *You can be any way you choose to be.*

Stop judging yourself or you could get depressed. And don't start judging yourself for judging yourself! The affirmation for this trick of the mind is: 'I'm judging myself again – and that's OK too.' Having seen what depression can do to people, how it saps the life-force and the will to live, I rejoice whenever I meet people who have a positive self-image. Britain has a low suicide rate compared with other countries –about 8.2 per 100,000 per year. It's still far too high. Let's all try to cut it down.

CHAPTER 9

Pulling your own strings

'Tis in ourselves, that we are thus or thus. Our bodies
are gardens, to the which our wills are gardeners.

Othello (I.iii)

It is common to hear people who are having trouble making
an important decision saying, 'a part of me wants to do this
but another part of me doesn't.' Often we feel split between
courses of action, have mixed feelings about people and
things, get confused by the different voices within us pulling
us in different directions. We say that a person has different
'sides' to his or her character, or 'is acting out of character',
'I don't know what came over me,' we protest, when we
feel ashamed of having behaved badly, that is, when one
part of us disapproves of the expression of another part
of us. As St Paul remarked wistfully, 'For the good that I
would I do not: but the evil which I would not, that I do.'
(Romans 7: 19). To feel truly in charge of our lives we need
to stop feeling controlled, manipulated, sabotaged or split
by parts of ourselves that remain in the unconscious. We
have to get to know who we are, and who we are is not just one
person but many.

Much of psychotherapy consists in uncovering patterns of
behaviour, often self-destructive, which seem to pursue their
own existence regardless of our conscious values and intentions. Beneath the one-tenth of the iceberg that is our
conscious mind, lie hidden the potentially manipulative
other nine-tenths, the subconscious and the unconscious,
containing the parts of us that we either are unaware of or
have rejected. Jungian analysis is largely about becoming
aware of how much we are influenced by disowned parts of

ourselves (our 'shadow') and by the archetypes of the Collective
Unconscious. Myth and literature abound in examples of the
power (sometimes demonic) of these disowned parts.
Caliban in *The Tempest* is Prospero's shadow, just as surely
as Mr Hyde is Dr Jekyll's or the picture is Dorian Gray's.
Danny Kaye's widow in an interview with the *New York
Times* once remarked about her husband that she couldn't
say what he was like in private life because 'there were too
many of him'.

Professor Robert Ornstein, the neurophysiologist who
wrote *The Psychology of Consciousness* and showed how left-
and right-side brains were specialized for different functions,
suggests that we are not one mind but many. Our brains have
many different compartments, each with minds of their own,
with one 'in charge' at any one time. Dr Hal Stone, an ex-
Jungian analyst living in Los Angeles, sees these 'minds' as
energies that we can harness for greater awareness and control of our lives. He developed a technique called 'Voice
Dialogue' in which the various parts are encouraged to speak
to us as if they were real people, telling us what they want,
how they try to get it, what fuels their energy. And indeed
these parts, or subpersonalities, do behave like real people
inside us, with consistent aims and styles of behaviour. If we
remain unconscious of them they will influence us too much,
sometimes disastrously, for their function is simply to push
us in the direction they want to go. Each subpersonality is
concerned only with its own needs and is totally unconcerned
with the needs of other subpersonalities or considerations of
practicality or appropriateness. Subpersonalities behave indeed like totally selfish, blinkered and demanding individuals. Allowed to take over, without the mediation of the
central 'I', they can tear us apart – and sometimes do. It is up
to us to make sure we stay in charge of our subpersonalities
and, while respecting them and listening to what they want,
do not let them run away with us, like a team of horses whose
driver has not kept a tight rein. It is the ego which must be the
decision maker, for it alone is in touch with external reality
and with what is appropriate. To change the metaphor, we
should be in relation to conflicting parts within us like a
chairman who, having listened to the various courses of

action proposed by delegates at a meeting, reserves the right
to the final decision.

Dr Stone's model is a useful one for understanding why
people act the way they do. For example, when we are finding
it hard to make a decision it is because two or more 'voices'
within us are urging different courses of action because each
sees the situation differently and wants different things.
When, for example, we make an irrational or disastrous
error of judgement it could be because temporarily we have
been seduced away from the dictates of common sense by
a part of us that is more interested in romance or adven-
ture than security or practicality. If we have got acquainted
with our many selves we are not so likely to be controlled
by them.

When making a decision, for example, we can listen in turn
to what each voice has to say, explore the assumptions of
each subpersonality, weigh up the sense of what we hear –
and then make our own decision on what is realistic. If,
another example, we are already aware of a part of us that is a
bohemian, hates routine, is lazy and hedonistic, we are less
likely when things are getting too hectic at work to blow a
fuse, hand in our resignation and 'drop out'. Respecting the
part of us that is feeling trapped and under stress, we can
instead arrange to take those days leave owing to us and take
off on a camping trip or otherwise give ourselves a break from
dull routine.

Listening to yourself, observing yourself in action, you will
get to recognize your main subpersonalities. They are legion,
for we are verily a crowd. Some will be very specific to yourself, but here are some that manipulate most of us.

The Critic

We have met the Critic already. He is the one who makes you
feel bad about yourself, never good enough, always wrong.
He is constantly comparing how it is with how it 'should' be,
how you are with how you ought to be. You can't win with the
Critic: whichever way you did it, it could have been done better
another way.

The Perfectionist

An ally of the Critic, the Perfectionist sees the world in terms of ideals and models to which he is constantly trying to make us measure up. He will let us die in the attempt if we let him.

The Workaholic

Let this one take over your life and you could be heading for a coronary or a divorce – or both. There simply is no end to this subpersonality's voraciousness for finding things for you to do. Try sitting down and relaxing and listen to its nagging voice starting straight away to remind you of those letters you should have written, those phone calls to be made, that ironing that has to be done, those invoices to be sent off, etc., etc. The voice is always urgent, and its purpose always to fill your time so that you never have a moment to relax.

The Pleaser

He's the one who makes us smile placatingly when we really feel angry, say 'sorry' when someone treads on our foot in a crowd, or 'no, thank you' to the last of the chocolates (even though we are lusting after it). Carole, the hairdresser we met in an earlier chapter, is totally manipulated by her Pleaser who makes it impossible for her to set boundaries to her giving, to say 'no' to people who are ripping her off. Not surprisingly, people like Carole store up a lot of anger behind their 'nice' façade, for their Pleaser will not allow them to be straight with others, to challenge them or to ask directly for what they want.

The Controller

The Controller's function is to keep us safe and protect us from doing anything that might threaten our self-image. This is the part of us that makes us freeze, cut off, or sulk when anyone has said anything to offend us, rather than expressing our displeasure or confronting the offender. The Controller feels threatened in any situation where spontaneity is called for, or the expression of feelings, in case we get out of control. It thus inhibits us from being authentic, 'letting our hair down', having fun, allowing ourselves to be just the way we are. It is the most uptight of all our subpersonalities. Its purpose is to protect. . . .

The Child

That the Child still lives in any of us is something of a miracle after the efforts that most of us have made to deny its existence because we are afraid of its vulnerability. Yet if we can acknowledge this vulnerability, we reclaim the other aspects of our Child: freshness, innocence, playfulness, spontaneity.

Is this you?

can't say no
unable to express your feelings
worried about what other people think
over-reacting without understanding why
behaving sometimes completely 'out of character'
can't relax
feeling insecure
having to fill every spare minute
always having to be in control
can't bear to be disliked
can't make up your mind
always too early
never on time
over-generous
obsessively mean
working harder than you need to
always needing approval from others
over-critical
always with more things to do
too hard on yourself
over-sensitive
smiling at people you don't like
unable to loosen up and enjoy yourself?

Before we go any further you might like to check out whether any of the subpersonalities described above is 'pulling your strings'.

See if you can work out which of your subpersonalities is in the driver's seat when you are in any of the above modes. *It is important to get to know your subpersonalities and what they want. They will help you make the right decisions.*

Sally and Johnny met at a London disco and clicked straightaway. They were both emerging from the breakdown of a marriage and licking their wounds, having been deserted by their partners for another. Johnny, a Dane, had taken a holiday in London to get away from the desolation of his empty flat in Copenhagen. Sally had allowed friends who knew how much she loved dancing to drag her out from moping at home to a disco.

They danced, talked, shared what was going on in their lives as if they had known each other for ages, found they thought alike on so many things, among them the sheer boringness of 'one-night stands' – and ended up in bed together. It was the beginning of a relationship that continued after Johnny's return to Copenhagen; letters, phone calls, return visits across the North Sea, meeting each other's friends and families and enjoying their approval and verdict that they were 'made for each other'.

Johnny has asked Sally to come and live with him in Copenhagen and is upset that she did not immediately agree.

But she is finding it hard to decide, for different parts of her are pulling her different ways. Her are some of the subpersonalities which are confusing Sally:

- her *woman* wants to be with her man and is saying *go!*
- her *child* is fearful to moving to a foreign country, of leaving her family and friends, of possibly being abandoned again – and is shrieking *don't go!*
- her *adventurous* side is excited at making a new start, getting out of a rut, learning a whole new way of life (*go!*)

- her *practical* side is worried about how she is going to live, since Johnny doesn't have much money. It tells her that Denmark is much more expensive than England, that she would be foolish to sell her flat, that it would be a hassle to rent it out, that she would have to give up her job etc., etc. (*don't go!*)
- her *pleaser* cannot bear to say 'no' to her lover and be disapproved of (*go!*)
- her *child* is fearful of being 'dropped' and being left alone again if she does not go.

Sally has to be careful to respect all these voices within her if she is going to stay in charge of her decision. If she allows one part to ride roughshod over the others they will give her no rest – and could sabotage her relationship one way of another. If she ignores the parts of her that want security and goes to Copenhagen she is likely to be anxious there, possessive, easily threatened, playing victim whenever they have an argument. ('Look what I gave up to be with you'). If, on the other hand, she lets the parts that want to play safe make the decision for her, she risks having her security but losing all the relationship has to offer her: intimacy, fun, challenge, a home with someone she loves.

She needs particularly to be aware of the vulnerable little girl inside her that is equally terrified of being surrounded by strangers in a foreign land as of being left alone in her own country. And, perhaps most of all, she needs to become aware of the part of her that thinks it has to do it all alone, cannot ask for support.

If Sally can share these parts of her with Johnny it will be easier for her to join him, feeling that she is being seen and heard, and not just uprooting herself to please him. It will also help him to understand her better and perhaps to give her child the reassurance she needs in order to feel safe enough to come over and be with him. *Subpersonalities may control you if you are not aware of them.*

Some subpersonalities are so over-developed that we identify with them, think they are 'us'. These lead us to choose one career rather than another, and the career then serves to strengthen this part of ourselves, sometimes to the point that we seem totally identified with it.

Frank has a strong *Controller* which has made him an effective classroom teacher. His lessons are always well-prepared, he keeps good order, enjoys his job. The trouble comes when he leaves school and goes home. He takes it with him. He gets irritated with his wife's lack of system in her housekeeping, his children's 'lack of discipline'. He has very set ideas on what is right and what is wrong, as if life were a multiple-choice question examination to be marked with a tick or a cross. He is terrified of any kind of spontaneity, which feels as threatening as if he were to turn up for a class unprepared. His intolerance of any kind of disagreement with his own views make him a bristly guest at dinner-parties and he has been known on ocasion to sulk like a child if his pronouncements are received with anything short of total attention and awe. Other adults are turned off by what comes over as a rigid, dogmatic and patronizing personality. Yet in fact it is a *sub*personality that Frank presents, is stuck in. He had a strict, puritanical upbringing by authoritarian parents who had sent him to a boarding school run by a religious order famed for its draconian discipline. In order to survive there he had to disown all the parts of him that did not fit in.

To be able to relax, to feel more at ease both with his family and in social relating, Frank needs to reclaim the parts of himself that were long ago buried because they were not rewarded, or brought disapproval and even punishment. He needs to give himself permission not to know the answers all the time, to allow a little sloppiness into his life, to be more playful, less serious, to maybe allow others to teach him something for a change – in short, to respect the child within him. But before this can happen he will have to re-experience the vulnerability and fear that made him bury the child in the first place and get to understand the suppressed panic that makes him need to be so controlling. But his whole life has been a denial of the part of him that is a little boy. His career has been partly a living out of his child through the class he teaches, and partly an attempt to feel in control of that child energy. If he manages to learn to value his own child energy, how he is at school will be subtly transformed. He will bring more freshness into his lessons, more humour, some love. He could then discover that perhaps his class has something to teach him.

Each job has its own *déformation professionelle* – the danger that we get so accustomed to using the part of us that can do the job well that we become it, even when we are not working. The solemnity of the priest, appropriate on the altar, only distances him from his parishioners when he is off it. The boss's command of what's going on in the office is admirable, but makes him a boring martinet at home. The cool, pleasant manner of the stewardess on the plane is professional; on the ground, merely plastic.

It is not that we have to try to get rid of any of the parts of ourselves. In fact, this would not be possible, for they are energies, and energy cannot be destroyed, only transformed. We saw in the last chapter that we will never get rid of anything we don't like in ourselves by fighting it, and this is true of subpersonalities. Disowning them merely drives them back into the unconscious where they will be even less under our control. Moreover, we *need* all our subpersonalities. They not only make us the unique beings that we are, but we developed them for specific purposes. Without our Controller, for example, we would never have survived so long: we would have been defenceless and crushed by life long ago. Without any Pleaser at all one would be boorish, totally devoid of any courtesy, grace or charm – and probably of friends as well. Without the energy that drives the Workaholic we would be layabouts, uncreative and unable to hold down a job at all or get anything done. Without allowing the Child in us expression our lives are dry, serious, joyless. But like real children the inner child needs us to set boundaries if it is to feel safe. If it is given too much space it will make it difficult for us to function in an adult society. We will be either far too vulnerable or far too irresponsible.

Some parts are overdeveloped and need boundaries setting to them, some are underdeveloped and need to be allowed more expression in our lives. Some are greedy and have become too fat, taking up too much space in our lives and always clamouring for attention. Others are starving for the chance to be expressed so that we can live up to our full potential. We have neglected these sides of ourselves so that they hardly have a voice at all, or, if they whisper, we do not hear them. We must honour all our selves. Each is like a player in an orchestra. We, as conductors, are responsible for keeping our selves in harmony and balance. It must be us, not they, who call the tune.

Disowned subpersonalities will haunt you

- Do you have a recurring dream?
- Do you have nightmares?
- Is there a particular type of person whom you cannot stand?
- Do you keep running into this type?
- Have you taken an instant dislike to someone without knowing why?
- Do you have an addiction that you hate but cannot break?
- Do you sometimes find yourself doing things you are really ashamed of?
- Do you sometimes feel impelled to do something, not knowing why?

Since our subpersonalities are types of energy, and since energy cannot be destroyed, they will not cease to exist just because we don't like them and disown them, that is, pretend to ourselves that 'we are not like that'. If we do not respect some parts of ourselves we create in ourselves parts that are not 'respectable', and, since we refuse to allow them into consciousness, beyond our control. We condemn them to an existence in a twilight world, longing for their place in the sun of conscious acceptance by the ego, to be allowed to take their place among the other 'respectable' parts of us and to be expressed in our lives. Just like people who have been rejected by society these 'misfits' can become rebellious and subversive and express themselves in ways that we find uncomfortable.

Whenever our conscious control is relaxed they can take us over. While we sleep, repressed instinctual energies appear in our dreams as animals, serpents, monsters. The greater the degree of conscious repression, the more terrifying the dream, of being pursued or devoured, for example. Jane had a recurring nightmare in which she was trying to dismember a monstrous black animal, half cat, half wallaby. In the dream she repeatedly hacked at it with a chopper, spraying the creature's blood over her clothes – but could never succeed in killing it. Jane had been brought up in the Outback of Australia in a redneck family. Her stepfather was ambitious for her and used to beat her to get her to do her homework. She hated him and looked rather to her grandfather for guidance. She remembered him impressing upon her that the way to get on in the world was always to be 'nice', ladylike. By sheer hard work she made it to university, took a science degree and escaped to Europe.

After travelling around, she settled in London, got herself a flat and found a job as a lab technician. She worked hard and eventually, due to her boss's high regard for her dedication, was put in charge of a research project. However, she was not happy. Not only did she have no life outside her work, but she was aware of the jealousy of the other members of the research team who had been there longer than she. One girl in particular showed hostility to her, Marie, whom Jane described as 'catty', 'tarty' and 'bitchy'. Jane had tried to win her over by being 'nice' but for once this was not working. That's when her nightmares had started and she decided to come to therapy.

The work in our sessions together turned out to be about reclaiming the parts of herself that had to be sacrificed in the interests of 'getting on' in the world. In order to please her stepfather and grandfather, Jane had to develop strongly three of her subpersonalities: the Good Student, the Dedicated Worker and the Nice Girl. She had worked on her Australian accent and become something of a culture snob to hide her feelings of inadequacy at her humble background. Pushed into the attic of her Unconscious were the earthier parts of herself and these were embodied in the creature in her dream, in which she enacted in symbolic form how she was living her life. She had been trying to kill her humble 'Australian' side (the wallaby) in order to become the sort of person she wanted to be, civilized and successful – 'European'.

Jane's associations with the cat in her dream were along the lines of 'selfish', 'could take or leave people', 'had claws, could scratch', 'catty' – in other words, the not-so-nice part of her.

As long as she rejected these parts of herself, not only would she be haunted by them in dreams, they would come at her too from the outside in other people. Jane now began to glimpse why she found Marie so disturbing. Her 'cattiness' was not only something Jane could not accept in herself, and therefore whose reflection was unsettling. The cat has also an extraordinary sensitivity to people's vibrations, and Jane instinctively knew that Marie could see through the façade of niceness with which Jane managed to disarm others. If Jane had had the courage to put aside her chopper and restore to health the poor tortured dream creature that was in fact herself she would be more whole and a whole lot happier. She might have learned to re-evaluate her Outback upbringing and to stop running away from it, to be more authentic and real, to draw on the cat's sensitivity and capacity to claw when in trouble. After all, wallabies and cats are cuddly animals, why kill them?

But she felt too threatened at the possibility that she may have been living a lie. She stopped coming to therapy and became a born-again Christian instead.

Jane will go on being disturbed by the Maries of this world until she stops projecting, and starts integrating her disowned subpersonalities, for whatever we deny in ourselves we will project outwards – and attract to ourselves like a magnet. Macho men will be homophobic, pacifists will attract violence, the ultra-virtuous will be endlessly shocked, the snob will be continuously offended by the 'naffness' of his fellow men. Much of racism is due to the threat of 'otherness', the fear of the 'black side' of our own natures. But black is not the colour of evil, black has simply been denied its place in the light of consciousness. Whenever we find ourselves using others as scapegoats, disliking them on sight, there is a part of ourselves that is presenting itself yet again to us to be reclaimed from our shadow that we may be more whole. It is in these little ways that love can replace hatred and intolerance, and the world itself, the macrocosm of the individual, can be at peace.

CHAPTER 10

Relating: A survival kit

'There lives within the very flame of love
A kind of wick or snuff that will abate it.'

Hamlet (IV.vii)

Playing the Victim Game in relationships is very popular because it is so easy. All you have to do is:

- idealize your partner
- rubbish your partner to anyone who will listen
- not say what you want and then blame your partner when things go wrong (Adam started this one)
- be totally convinced you alone are right (the 'Othello syndrome')
- be totally convinced you alone are wrong and get depressed
- play helpless and then react against feeling uncomfortably dependent
- try to live up to your partner's expectations
- expect your partner to live up to yours
- insist on being always in control and then complain that you never feel held
- expect your partner to know what you need and then sulk if they don't
- give out of a sense of duty (the martyr syndrome) and then throw it in his or her face in an argument
- take your partner for granted and then weep bitter tears when they go off with someone who doesn't.

If you find yourself playing any of these games in a relationship, at least comfort yourself with the idea that you

have managed to let another human being get through to you
– something never achieved by many people. You *are*
involved, you *can* be vulnerable, you *do* feel. It is very probable that in every relationship that has proceeded beyond
the superficial stages, in every marriage after the honeymoon
phase has worn off, one or other (or on a bad night, both)
partners will on occasion find themselves sleepless at the
furthest edge of the bed thinking 'What on earth am I *doing*
with this creep?' Angry or depressed at the sheer awfulness
of your partner, remembering the harsh, half-meant words
flung at each other, miserable, feeling very alone again, you
listen to the alarm clock's loud tick or, much worse, the
regular breathing that means your partner has managed to
get off to sleep. You would like to cross the no man's land that
yawns between you both and bridge it with a cuddle . . . but
you don't dare to, either proud, wanting revenge or fearful of
being rejected.

The greatest emotional stress a human being can experience,
from infancy to old age, is loss of love. We need it to survive,
literally. Traumatized by separation and loss, children may
not thrive, discarded lovers can become seriously depressed,
the widowed often lose their will to go on living. Our bitterest
experiences very often are of love turned sour, of discord,
guilt and betrayal, of memories, now it's all over, of good
times together. The need for love is primary, the loss of it
devastating.

Intimate relationships, when they are functioning well, are
bliss. When they are going badly they are sheer hell. Money,
power, fame, prestige, aristocratic status are no protection
against heartache. Even royalty can have a hard time with
their relationships. Henry VIII played victim to six wives in
turn. He complained that they were either unproductive,
unfaithful, too ugly or too Protestant. Even 'Sweet Jane'
went and died on him. Edward II's marriage to Isabella of
France ended up for the King as rather more than a pain in
the neck, while that of Darnley to Mary, Queen of Scots was
sheer murder, too. George IV refused to share his coronation
with his Queen and left her banging in frustration on the locked
doors of Westminster Abbey, while Edward VIII cancelled
his because his wife wasn't invited. The relationship prob-

lems of the rich and famous fascinate us simply because we can relate to them.

There are as many possible types of relationship as there are combinations of individuals. There is no such thing as a 'normal' pairing between consenting adults, for every relationship is unique. Whatever our colour, status, gender, we are all seeking escape from our emotional isolation, to find a soul-mate, to give and receive love, to be seen and heard, to share our lives. Black, brown, pink or yellow, rich or poor, heterosexual or homosexual, we seek fulfilment in the only way we know how. Inside every nagger, controller, manipulator and tantrum-thrower is a frustrated soul, a vulnerable and potentially caring human being who does not feel nourished.

There will surely be times in every relationship when some suffering is unavoidable. Times, for example, of enforced separation for whatever reason; of having to watch your partner coping with a bad time, in pain or bereavement; sadness when there is a genuine failure to meet each other's needs, or some irreconcilable difference between you. But, remember, it is not the acceptance of unavoidable suffering that makes one a victim. Where you are *not* in charge is when your needs are not being met and you do not ask youself why, and what you can do about it.

Alas, just to 'be in love' is not enough. Without awareness, love truly can be blind. We can end up stumbling in the debris of shattered dreams wondering what hit us – or, worse, why – after we gave so much. Just as awareness without love can be cold and heartless, so love without awareness can be manipulative and destructive. They need each other just as surely as the two wings of a plane need each other. Without them both you will have a hard time even getting off the ground – let alone getting high together. So, if you are unhappy in your relationship it's up to you to take a good look at what is actually going on between the two of you in the name of love. There could be some games going on that you are unaware of – and could even get to enjoy them if you knew what they were.

The first step in changing anything for the better is, as usual, to look into why any change is necessary and what it is exactly that needs changing.

What's missing in your relationship?

good sex	humour
security	mutual respect
intimacy	commitment
affection	sharing
touching and being touched	appreciation
warmth	loyalty
honesty	trust
communication	more time together
physical contact	more time apart?
understanding	

How to stop being a victim in relationships

Start by taking responsibility for having chosen this partner in the first place and for staying with him or her. Then check for areas where you may be giving or receiving double messages, playing games, getting trapped in roles, or simply unaware of how you give your power away. Here are some common sources of knots, crossed lines and distortion in communication which make it hard to see and hear each other and make for misunderstandings and resentment in close relationships.

Projections and roles

These get in the way of seeing each other as we really are and make us relate to the other person as if they were somebody else. We attribute intentions and motives to them that have more to do with us than with them. Here are some of the common roles we project on to our beloveds and then get trapped into relating to them only in a certain way. They may even be why we chose them as partners in the first place.

Parent
More likely to be your projection on your partner if he or she is older than you, and even more so if they have personality traits that remind you of your father or your mother.

Anna is a concert violinist, talented and exotically beautiful. She is in her late twenties and met Philip at a party after one of her concerts. He is in his late fifties, rich, very distinguished looking, with a mane of white hair. He was attentive and very flattering about her performance, and sensitive enough to her fatigue after performing to protect her from gushing admirers at the party and to drive her home as soon as she started talking about leaving. In the next few weeks he courted her in a way that won her heart, telephoning daily, sending flowers with romantic messages, attending her next concert. She accepted his invitation to go and relax at his house in the country, where they became lovers.

For six months it was idyllic. Philip saw it as his role to shield Anna from the petty hassles of life so that she could be free to concentrate on her art, to practise and prepare for her next concert. He advised her on everything, from how to invest her money to what she should wear. He bought her new clothes, delighted in showing her off, took her to expensive restaurants, paid for her lessons. At first she loved being taken care of in this way. It was a new experience for her. Her parents had separated when she was very young, after which she had seen little of her father, who was something of a ladies' man, while her mother had depended heavily on her for emotional support. As a student she had lived in Paris on a pittance and had been very lonely, spending her time either at violin lessons or practising many hours a day in her room. This relationship was her first experience of feeling held and cared for. For her Philip represented the Good Father she had never had and she became very dependent on him.

Because of her abandonment as a child by her real father, however, Anna felt insecure about the permanence of their relationship. She started to hint to Philip that she wanted a baby, perhaps they should get married. Philip at first headed her off, then when she kept returning to the subject, would become irritated. He took to going away 'on business' and would be away for days, during which she felt like an abandoned child, waiting anxiously for his return and needing a lot of reassurance when he did that he still loved her. She feels he is beginning to get bored with her, making love less often and only to please her. She is desperate, not knowing what to do to keep him. He is becoming more and more critical of her. Whatever she says or does now seems only to irritate him. He is turning, for her, into the Bad Father whom she has to placate if he is not to go away and leave her.

In any close relationship our 'unfinished business', the unresolved conflicts and unmet needs from the past tend to come to the surface as projections that have to be understood and withdrawn if we want an adult, equal relationship with our partner. Men turn their wives into mothers and then wonder either where the sexual energy between them went or why the women lose their respect for them or get to resent them for being so needy. Unless, of course, their wives need to play the role of Mother, perhaps either to avoid sexuality or to control their man by pandering to his Child.

Child

Mary was the oldest of a large family and so was used to having to look after her younger brothers and sisters. Her relationships with men have followed the same pattern and have all been disastrous. She is always attracted to the same type of man: charming, playful – and quite irresponsible. It is the Child in them that 'hooks' her, for, having always had to shoulder responsibility, she has never really been allowed to be a child herself. Her lovers have led her a merry dance. They have lied to her, borrowed money from her and never repaid it, left their jobs as soon as they started to live with her, sat around the flat all day smoking dope or sipping beer in front of the television while she's out earning the rent. But because they make her laugh, show her how to relax, she can not be hard on them, preferring to be hard on herself to make it possible for them to play together. She is living out her own disowned Child subpersonality through them – and being ripped off in the process.

Transactional analysis is based on the premise that in each of us there is a Parent, an Adult and a Child. In any inter-action between two adults they may not in fact be relating to each other as adults. One or both of them may be assuming the role of the Parent (controlling, judgemental, protective) or the role of the Child (fearful, dependent, irresponsible,

playful, rebellious). Next time you have a heated argument
with your partner, try to become aware of which of you is slip-
ping into the Parent role (who is laying down the law or coming
on heavy?) and who is taking up a Child position ('it wasn't
my fault' – or whoever throws the tantrum or bursts into
tears). If you can both manage to retrieve the Adult position
then you stand a good chance of sharing what you both want
and how you feel you are not being seen or heard by the other.
Characteristic of the Adult position is this sharing of what's
going on with you rather than blaming the other person. If
you stay with talking about your own feelings rather than
dumping negativity on the other, they are less likely to feel
threatened and go into their Outraged Parent or Hurt
Child.

Disowned subpersonalities

We saw in the last chapter how parts of ourselves that we do
not express become projected on others. This happens very
commonly in relationships. Without perhaps being aware of
it, the other partner will pick up the projection and start living
it out. It is as if we unconsciously invite the other to behave in
a certain way and then polarize against it. It is no accident
that Mary's boyfriends stop working as soon as they get
involved with her. She is broadcasting the message 'I want to
look after you' and turning them into children in her unconscious search for someone who will teach her how to play.

Martin came for therapy because he was confused about
his relationships. He had left Angela, his wife, because he
could not stand her emotional scenes any more. She was constantly 'picking on him', 'throwing tantrums', 'doing her nut'
and 'flying off the handle' over nothing in particular – in
short, 'being totally unreasonable'. He was seeing Susan, who
was in love with him, and contrasted her gentle, loving ways
with those of his virago of a wife. Yet he would not go to live
with Susan, preferring instead to rent a flat. Every weekend
he would go back and stay with his wife, claiming that he did
so 'to keep her quiet' as she repeatedly rang him at work to
ask when he was coming home.

As our sessions unfolded, Martin's difficulty in expressing
himself became very apparent, as did his lack of confidence.

He revealed that he had had a reputation before he married for being 'a bit of a stud' because he only went in for 'one-night stands'. Wryly, he confessed that the reason he would never see a girl again was his fear of her getting to know what he was really like, insecure, inarticulate, emotionally frozen. He felt he had nothing of value to give any woman and was terrified that intimacy would reveal his emptiness. Angela had pursued him and he had married her as an escape from the danger of any real involvement since 'she wasn't very bright' and would, he thought, be content with the material things he could give her (he had inherited his father's business and was quite well off). After a few years of relating 'reasonably well' it became evident that they could not have children and things began to change. She began making emotional demands on him to which he could not respond. This was when the tantrums started and he eventually moved out and into the flat to escape.

Martin was repeatedly evasive when I asked him why, if the weekend visits to his wife were so traumatic and unpleasant, he did not stop going. Why, too, if Susan nourished him and cared for him, did he not move in with her? He talked about feeling guilty about having left Angela and about how she could not survive without him, as if she were a vulnerable child. This was certainly not the impression I had formed of her from his account. It seemed more like she had the power and he was the child. One weekend he called round as usual and he was quite put out when she remarked casually that she was going to a party that night. We worked on his reaction in the next session and it became clear that he was being repeatedly drawn back to his wife, not to 'save her going potty' as he had put it, but because *he* needed to 'go home'.

Gradually the real dynamics of Martin's relationship with both Angela and Susan emerged. He had projected his dis-owned side on to his wife who was thus landed with carrying the emotional energy in their marriage. Without knowing why, she found herself repeatedly over-reacting, trying to 'get through' his schizoid barriers to anything but superficial and 'reasonable' relating. Martin's feeling of guilt was not, as he thought, at leaving her alone, but the dimly-felt realization that he had never loved her and was incapable of any real feeling about anyone. This was why he was ambivalent about Susan. He enjoyed her adoration but feared that closer intimacy with her would show up his emotional bankruptcy. While complaining about Angela's outbursts he was, in fact, living out his disowned side through her and, on an energy level, colluding with them. Separating completely from her would have cut him off from this vicarious experiencing of vitality and would have made him feel even more dead inside.

When two people are living together they will influence each other deeply at an unconscious level and start responding to what is latent or unexpressed in the other. Whatever a relationship becomes, it is always a joint creation. It is a dance, and it takes two to tango. There are no persecutors without willing victims. And trying to be the perfect partner is guaranteed to bring out the worst in your other half, for saints only create sinners. If you feel constantly irritable or unworthy in your relationship for no apparent reason it is just possible that you are carrying your partner's disowned negativity. If you hate yourself for behaving badly when you don't mean to, you may well be acting out his or her shadow side.

One of the ways couples polarize is in the area of control and vulnerability. Sandra is thinking of leaving Jeremy after a relationship lasting four years. It is a hard decision to make, for in many ways they get on well together. They share particularly a love of the country, spending most weekends in the cottage that Jeremy owns in the Cotswolds, enjoying riding, long walks, having friends down from London from time to time. Sandra will miss that and the fun they have when things are going well. But when things are not going well she cannot bear the way Jeremy closes off from her and seems to withdraw to some place within himself that she cannot reach. It happens equally if things are not going well for him or for her. She complains to her friends that, if she is feeling distressed or vulnerable, there is no way she can share it with Jeremy. He just doesn't want to know and avoids the situation by making himself busy, going out on his own, or, even worse, suggesting that she 'takes things too seriously'. He will not share with her, either, his own vulnerability. If he has a problem, he sorts it out himself and never discusses it with her.

We bring to a new relationship the lessons we have learned in former ones – and the scars. Jeremy was divorced, with three teenage children. He had been a doctor in general practice. His ex-wife, Jean, had been a nagger and complainer, always discontented, which is why he had eventually left her for Sandra who was 'fun to be with'. Jeremy was sick to death of having to listen to complaints both in the surgery and at home, of being around 'moaners'. He had had it all his life, for his mother, too, was unhappy in her marriage and made her children feel guilty at separating from her. Whenever Sandra was feeling down or wanted some support from her lover she became for Jeremy one of the 'moaners' he thought he had escaped from – and he would escape again by withdrawing his energy from her. Jeremy has never experienced anyone 'holding' him, containing his vulnerability, so he has had to do it himself all his life by being very controlled. This control is threatened when Sandra expects him to share his vulnerability with her. His pathology consists of his defences against his own vulnerability and his paranoia about any emotional demands being made upon him that will make him feel helpless, trapped or guilty again. These two people have different expectations from their relationship. Sandra expects to be allowed to give and feel support in the bad times as well as enjoying the good times. Jeremy denies the bad times, wants only the fun times. It stops them going any deeper together, which stores up resentment, which is why the relationship is in trouble.

Togetherness versus space

In every love relationship (as, indeed, in every close association between people) there are two conflicting dynamics pulling us in different directions. They are:

- the desire to merge with the other
- the need to feel one's separateness.

To feel totally open to another human being, to feel that

there are no barriers between you, to relax into each other, is what makes the difference between sex and making love, between mere pleasure and bliss. It is a heady potion – and we can become addicted to it. We miss it when it is not there and assume something is wrong when either of us wants to be alone. But there is a difference between saying, 'I don't want to be with you right now,' and 'I need to be with myself right now.' The former is a rejection, the latter is simply respecting the need to recharge one's batteries, to come back into one's self again. It is the natural rhythm of coming together and drawing apart again. The secret of living together harmoniously is being sensitive to each other's space and respecting it. When two people are really in tune they know the art of being together yet enjoying their own space, perhaps reading, listening to music or simply relaxing contentedly while the partner does his or her own thing, perhaps in the same room, perhaps not. It is not always necessary to be talking to be in contact.

These times of aloneness in a relationship refresh us and make us more totally involved in the times when we are together. It may well be true that we are not ready to be in a relationship until we can really enjoy being alone. To go into a relationship merely to escape from being alone or from loneliness (not the same thing) rather than because you want to be with *this* person. This is not a recipe for success. It is as doomed as getting married because you want to escape from your family. A strain is put on the relationship, either by your clinging or by your fear of losing your individuality by becoming too dependent on the other.

Expectations

No one person can satisfy all your needs. There are some things you will have either to give to yourself or to get from others. Sometimes you will be there for each other, but sometimes you won't, with the best will in the world. In times of crisis it might help to remind yourself that, lovers though you may be, you remain separate people. When you are furious that your expectations have not been met, or feeling guilty at

not wanting to meet your partner's, remind yourself of this
'Gestalt prayer':

> I am not in this world to meet your expectations.
> You are not in this world to meet mine.
> I am here to do my thing.
> You are here to do your thing.
> Sometimes we will meet – and that's beautiful.
> Sometimes we won't. Too bad.

Yes, it is a little hard, not very loving. But it is a reminder that
it is nobody else's responsibility to make us happy but our
own, and also not to take blissful togetherness as the norm
and to assume something is wrong with our relationship when
it's not happening. The norm is our separateness, our aloneness. Any bliss we may experience with another is a blessing
to be grateful for and to treasure. Don't be greedy or you will
kill the golden-egg-laying goose.

CHAPTER 11
Learning to trust

There's place and means for every man alive.

All's Well That Ends Well IV. iii

The master keys to taking charge of our life are cultivating more *awareness* and realizing that we always have *choice*. They restore to us a sense of inner freedom and unlock the closed doors that may have been barring our way to better health, inner peace and more satisfying relationships. If we have the courage and honesty (or are sufficiently desperate) to really look at our lives, to stop behaving mechanically out of habit and conditioning, to take responsibility for what we get and start creating what we want, we can never again feel victimized by anyone or anything. As Colin Wilson puts it:

> We *must* grasp this central fact: that most of our problems are self-inflicted, caused by 'negative feedback'. We allow some dreary prospect to cause a sinking feeling, then accept the sinking feeling as evidence that life is difficult and dangerous – 'We can't win'. Our descendants will look back with astonishment on our naïvety. They will have learned the crucial lesson: that external events may or may not be controllable; *we* choose our reaction to them.'
>
> (*Access to Inner Worlds*)

Staying in charge of our lives calls for constant vigilance against this tendency of our minds to see things negatively and the self-limiting patterns it tries to impose upon us. This is the essence of the teaching of enlightened masters, the 'mindfulness' of the Buddha, the 'self-remembering' of

Gurdjieff, the 'watch and pray' of Jesus. *Whenever we identify with our minds we are in for trouble.* We are not our minds. In fact, if you observe, there is no such thing as 'mind'. It is not an entity but a constantly changing process – a procession of thoughts that come and go like bubbles on the breeze. To meditate is simply to practise watching these bubbles without becoming enveloped by them, becoming trapped in the view of reality that each represents. In this way the meditator becomes grounded in the witnessing 'I', the Watcher, Pure Awareness, Subjectivity, the Space in which the thought-bubbles come and go. This is inner freedom – freedom from the negative emotions that are generated by becoming 'hooked' into negative thinking and which in turn generate negative actions and responses; freedom to choose positive thought forms to raise our energy levels and to enjoy life more and to cope with the challenges it gives us.

By seeing, feeling, responding and acting according to which thought forms we are holding on to, we create our own level of reality, attracting the experiences appropriate to that level. *If you see yourself as a victim you will create persecutors in your life.* People and things only have the power over you that *you* give to them.

Are you, for example, like many people, the victim of money? Do you give it the power to make you:

- anxious
- envious
- paranoid
- desperate
- prostitute yourself
- poison your relationships
- ruin your health through over-working?

Very few people are clear about money. Can you, for example:

- accept with grace others' insistence on footing the bill
- ask for a loan if you are broke
- refuse to be manipulated into giving money if you don't want to

- ask for money back that is owed to you
- negotiate a fair price for something you are selling
- decide how much you need and how you are going to make it
- turn down offers of money because of the strings attached?

What are your basic assumptions about money?

that is it hard to come by

that one man's gain is another man's loss

that it has to be worked hard for

that it is 'uncool' to have or to be concerned about

that it is essential to have a lot of it in order to be happy

that it is a curse – the 'root of all evil'

that if you don't have much of it you are a nobody

that money 'talks'

that if you had more of it all your problems would be solved

that there can be no sense of security without it

that if you were to lose it all you might as well commit suicide?

It is easier to lower one's sights than to win the pools, and if we have made our happiness conditional on being rich, what we get if we are poor is conditioned misery. If we are well off, but have to punish our bodies or sell our souls to stay that way, we are not really as well off as we think. The point, if we do not want money to control us, is not whether any of the above assumptions are right or wrong, but to become aware of how they make us act and how they are affecting the way we live now.

The bottom line with money, as with relationships and health, is fear. Fear of poverty, of not being fed, of having nobody to look after us in our old age, of ending up destitute – or, if we *have* money, fear of losing it from anything from burglary or mugging to unwise investment or collapse of the market. The greed in the world arises from fear of deprivation, that there is not enough to go round, so it's every man

for himself. This fear affects governments as well as
individuals, for it is a collective phenomenon. What, after all,
is an 'arms race' but paranoia at the highest level?

If we are to stay in charge of our lives we will have to be
continually confronting our fear. If we are to stay in charge of
our lives we must not let fear take control of our thinking,
feelings, actions and relationships. Fear makes us tense,
stifles creativity and innovation, the playfulness and curiosity
out of which so often new discoveries are stumbled upon,
whether about ourselves or the universe. Fear stops us being
open to and with others, inhibits us from being ourselves,
makes us intolerant of differences whether of colour, creed or
gender, engendering both the coldness and violence in the
world. Our ultimate fear is the fear of death. It lies behind the
fear of poverty, of being abandoned, of nothingness, of
letting go.

When you have learned to live with your existential fear –
and live your life to the full in spite of it – you have taken
charge of your life. You will grow through taking risks and
learning from confronting what it is you fear most. Individuation, becoming more fully who you are, achieving quality in
your life, freedom and fulfilment, is not cheap. It has to be
worked for. It takes courage, it takes guts. And it helps a lot if
you can trust.

What do we need to learn to trust if we are to be able to
conquer our fear? What thought forms do we need to choose
instead of the paranoia of our minds that makes us victims of
stale and mediocre living, that would have us make ourselves
'secure' at all costs, hanging on grimly to the dead past, insuring
anxiously against the future, threatened by anything fresh,
new and unexpected, in other words, Life?

We need to learn to trust ourselves

Trusting ourselves is not something we have been taught, so
it is something we have to learn. We have to learn to trust our
intuition, the part of us that knows, our innate wisdom. We
have to stop looking outside ourselves for the truth, imitating
others, manipulating ourselves to 'fit in' and be one of the

crowd of people who are as unsure as we are. We have to go against the conditioning that has taught us that there are 'right' feelings and 'wrong' feelings, 'good' thoughts and 'bad' thoughts, 'normal' and 'abnormal' behaviour. Rather, we should constantly search inside ourselves for what is authentic and accept it unconditionally, let it guide us in the next way to move, rely on our awareness and sensitivity to show us how to respond appropriately to the situations we find ourselves in. We all have this 'inner guide' but its voice is gentle and we have been deafened to it by the stridency of other voices outside us that confuse us and take us away from ourselves. We have to learn again the art of listening, to our bodies and to our hearts rather than to our minds, which are merely the sum total of our conditioning. The more we trust our intuition, the surer it grows.

Our intuition will tell us when we need exercise and when we need to rest and give us early warning of things not being as they should be with our health. More sensitivity will sweeten our relationships, for we will sense the times to communicate and the times to be silent, the times for getting close and the times for putting space between us. We will know when output of energy is called for to further our projects – and when it is rather a time for waiting, for drawing in our horns and lying fallow.

> To every thing there is a season, and a time to every
> purpose under the heaven.
>
> (*Ecclesiastes, 3: 1*)

Trust your right-side brain to show you *timing* and to tune in to the real behind appearances.

Don't try to be consistent. Consistency is another name for inflexibility. If you are truly living in the present, which is constantly changing, you will necessarily change with it. It is like driving: sometimes it will be appropriate to accelerate, sometimes to slow down or to stop. Trying to live your life out of habit and past experience is like driving along looking only in the rear view mirror rather than adapting your driving to what's coming ahead – and then wondering what hit you.

There is a Zen story of the master who was asked by a

disciple how he should live his life. The master held out his open hand and asked the disciple, 'What would you say if my hand was always like this?' The disciple, a little uncertainly, replied, 'That it was deformed.' 'Very good,' said the master, now clenching his hand into a fist. 'And what would you say if my hand was always like this?'

'The same, that it was deformed.'

'Very true,' said the master, 'so don't live a deformed life.'

Zen abhors rules, programmes, imitation, second-hand living. It has only one discipline – that of spontaneity, freshness, authentic responses arising from a present-centred awareness of what is going on around us. Zen was the flowering, the coming together of Taoism and Buddhism. The last words of the Buddha were 'Be a Light unto yourself.' The Taoist sage Lao-Tsu put it this way:

A man is born gentle and soft.
At his death he is stiff and hard.
Green plants are tender and full of sap.
Dead, they are dry and withered.
Therefore the stiff and inflexible is the disciple of death.
The gentle and yielding, the disciple of life.

(*Tao Te Ching*, Chapter 76)

We need to learn to trust life

Trusting your inner guide and trusting life are the same thing, for we are not separate from life. The higher religions, meditation, certain forms of yoga, paths to enlightenment, all aim at developing this realization that we are all parts of the Whole, at freeing us from the paranoia that goes with seeing ourselves as isolated individuals, aliens in a universe that appears uncaring, sometimes hostile, always indifferent. The good news is that, tiny though we are in a vast cosmos, we are not merely particles of conscious matter that 'just happened' to evolve at random on this particular planet. Quantum physics is discovering that, far from being a random universe, it is an ordered one that seems deliberately to have set things up the way they are, to have *chosen* it the way it is. Selecting and rejecting possibilities over millennia, the universe prepared the way for our coming by evolving the optimum conditions of life to survive on earth – and then gave birth to humankind. It wanted us here and goes on nourishing us because it wants us to go on being here.

For some 'It' is 'Our Father', for others, the 'Great Mother' or the nameless Tao, 'beginning of heaven and earth'. Yet others see It as Absolute Consciousness or the Holy Spirit, the Eternal Principle. Whatever 'It' is, It knows we are here because It put us here. And perhaps there is less space between It and us than we think. What exactly is meant by saying we are made 'in God's image', for example? Who are we really? If you can crack that one you get a prize for becoming enlightened. Perhaps what makes it such a hard one to fathom out is that we may be trying to separate the Dancer from the Dance. In other words, perhaps we are one with It, and each of our lives a part of Its Dance.

It is not important that we should all see It in the same way (and would that the world could at last agree on this!), so much as that we each of us make our own relationship with It (whatever It is) and trust in Its benevolence. We must learn to draw strength and inspiration from It (what used to be called 'grace') in the same way as we draw breath. Rather than trying to control life we should be trying to understand its ways and living in harmony with It by mastering our minds. Above all, we have to stop relating to It as if It were out to get us, our enemy, rather than It as, to use the Bishop of Woolwich's phrase, the 'Ground of Our Being'. In order not to be a victim to fear, trust, not insurance, is the key. It will make all the difference to how we are in the world, how we face any *unavoidable* suffering that life brings us, if we trust, deep down, when all seems to be falling apart, the revelation to the medieval mystic, Julian of Norwich:

All is well, and all manner of thing shall be well . . .

The universe, like the individual psyche, appears to be self-regulating. Life is an interplay of opposite and balancing forces. Any movement too far in one direction is corrected by a swing to the other, rather like the pendulum of a grandfather clock. Avoid extremes of any kind and you will avoid any backlash. And if you have gone too far out in one direction, probably through attachment or lack of awareness, trust that the suffering brought you by that backlash will soon burn itself out if you have the patience to stay with it rather than trying to avoid the effects of your unwise actions. Trust the way energy is flowing and flow with it rather than resisting it. Taking charge of our lives is ultimately about seeing into the laws of cause and effect and living in harmony with them to avoid giving yourself a bad time.

Life is paradoxical. We have to try to change the things that make for unhappiness and stagnation in our lives in order not to be victims. At the same time, we have to cultivate acceptance of the 'will of God' and trust the direction that life is taking us in. And perhaps the biggest paradox of all is that if, having tried to change that which cannot be changed, we choose to surrender, we stay in charge of our lives.

CHAPTER 12
The energy game

This above all – to thine own self be true,
And it must follow, as the night the day,
Thou can'st not then be false to any man.

Hamlet (I.iii)

The idea linking all the chapters in this book is that of energy awareness. If we want to take charge of our life we have to stop playing the Victim Game and start playing the Energy Game – with awareness. We have to become aware of the quality of the energy we have been taking in and the quality of the energy we have been putting out – and take responsibility for the quality of life we have (or do not have).

We need to think of ourselves in terms of constantly changing energy-spaces and our relationships more in terms of dynamic energy transactions instead of as fixed entities. We need more understanding and less labelling of our feelings, our needs – and, indeed, those of others – and to accept and respect them without being controlled or driven by them. In order not to be manipulated into putting up with what we don't want – and then complaining about it – we have to be sufficiently in touch with what we *do* want and with our own capacity to mobilize our resources to make it happen. In the process, we have to be prepared to look at our attachments and our investment in being a victim and the ways in which we limit ourselves. Above all, we have to learn to contact and trust that part of us that knows what is right for us and harness it to the power we all have to create what we want in our lives.

This way of seeing ourselves in terms of changing energy states is more than just a useful working model. If we observe, we will see that, whatever else humans have in common with each other, we are in fact all engaged from moment to moment in energy transformation. We take in raw materials (air, food) and convert them into the energy we need for living, i.e., for thinking, feeling, sensing, moving, acting. We can either do all these things like robots, automatically and sometimes (unconsciously) selfdestructively, or we can bring more awareness to them to create more *quality* in our lives. More and more of us, for example, have started doing this already at a basic level by ensuring we get enough exercise, do not smoke, and eat the right foods to stay healthy – in other words, improving the quality of the raw materials we take in. The less automatic we become, the more we realize that we can choose what other forms of energy we take in and what we put energy into, what we give our attention to – which thoughts and feelings we dwell on for example. Taking charge of our lives becomes more and more and more about exercising this muscle of choice.

The first choice that has to be made in order to move out of the Victim Game is to stop giving yourself – and others – a hard time and to start to nourish yourself at all levels, bodily, mentally, emotionally and spiritually.

This final chapter is an invitation to go on co-operating with the ever-changing energy process that you are, becoming more conscious and more sympathetic to it, of riding your life the way it is going and enjoying the ride rather than being dragged along because you refuse to sit in the saddle and take the reins. The more one gets accustomed to thinking in terms of energy and the more sensitive one gets to energy states in oneself and others, the more sensitive one becomes to imbalances and staleness, being in a rut, or negativity, or when energy levels are getting run-down. Knowledge is power, and knowing oneself is empowering. One does not wait until one is in a crisis situation as regards health, emotional state, relationships or money, and then panic, blame or complain. If one constantly works with energy to *create*, one is spared having to *cope*.

Never before in history, have so many resources for transforming one's awareness and energy states been so widely available as are today, for those interested in working on themselves. As more and more people start taking responsibility for their own well being, the number of popular publications to do with health proliferate. Increasingly, we are made aware of the interconnection of mind and body and offered a range of approaches to heightening well being geared to one or the other. Alternative practitioners are flourishing as never before, vegetarianism is no longer considered 'cranky', yoga and meditation no longer 'esoteric' but practised routinely by large numbers of 'ordinary' people.

Listed below are some of the resources available for helping you in the 'Energy Game' when you feel your energy (or awareness) needs clearing, boosting, balancing or centering. What they have in common is that they are all holistic in approach, see well being, or absence of it, in terms of the state of our energy, whether it is balanced, flowing, blocked, or stagnating. They all aim to transform our energy state in some way, either by working directly with body energies or with energies on subtler mental, emotional and spiritual planes. We should think of them not as 'alternative' therapies, but as *complementary* to orthodox medicine. Your medical practitioner should, of course, be consulted first if you are worried about your health. Our intention here is not to describe in detail how they work so much as to provide a guideline as to how they could be usefully explored for the area in which you need to do some work on yourself. Some of them in any case will already be familiar to you and books on them are readily available. The author has restricted the list of resources to ones that he has personally experienced and found useful in moving energy at various times when he has felt 'stuck'. Readers interested in knowing more about them can do so by consulting both the author's *How To Beat Fatigue* (Arrow 1987) and *The Alternative Health Guide* by Brian Inglis and Ruth West (Michael Joseph 1983). Both books also list contact addresses for following-up.

In crisis situations

Counselling
Knowing when you need professional advice and support, and where to go for it, is not inconsistent with taking charge

of your life. It involves knowing what you need, being aware of your own lack of technical knowledge or expertise – and mobilizing the resources in your environment which can provide these. There are times – of loss or bereavement, for example – when some form of short-term counselling will help you cope with distress and accept the bitter cup life is offering you right now. Or it may be that your problem is a medical one, or financial or legal. Consult the experts rather than agonizing alone and getting depressed. That's what they are there for. Help them make a living. Often, if you know where to look, you can get the advice you need for free, or for a contribution.

Positive thinking

Much of the tension of a crisis situation arises from our negative feelings about it that can tempt us back into playing the Victim Game. Resist the temptation – it will only make things worse than they are already. Once you have done everything you can to contain or improve the objective situation, put your energy into examining what exactly this situation means to you, what is so painful or anxiety-producing about it. Bring more awareness to exactly what catastrophic expectations your mind is coming up with – and if they are unrealistic (and they usually are!), change them with positive visualizations and affirmations as described in earlier chapters. Remind yourself that, however dire things appear, 'This too shall pass', as it always has done in the past. And when it does, give yourself credit for having met yet another challenge successfully and being left stronger as a result – which is perhaps why you had to go through it in the first place. To learn more techniques for more positive and creative thinking, you could sign up for a course in one of the following. What they have in common is the replacement of self-limiting programmes in our mind-computers with ones which are more likely to generate the energies and attract the experiences we need for more quality in our lives.

- Silva mind control
- Neuro-linguistic programming (NLP)
- Prosperity consciousness.

For dispelling negative states
Bach Flower Remedies
Dr Edward Bach gave up a lucrative Harley Street practice to devote his time to finding plant remedies which would heal physical illness, which, he believed, was always the result of underlying negative emotional states. The 38 remedies, derived from flowering plants, cover every known negative state, so you can rest assured that the one that happens to be plaguing you will be be among them. They range from Remedy number 1, *Agrimony* ('for those who suffer considerable inner torment which they try to dissemble behind a façade of cheerfulness'), to number 38, *Willow* ('resentment and bitterness, with 'not fair' and 'poor me' attitudes'). Try that one if you're playing the Victim game! The 'Rescue Remedy' (number 39) is a combination of remedies for use in times of crisis and shock, for example, when overcome by grief. All the Bach remedies and where to get them are listed in *How to Beat Fatigue* (pp. 99–101).

Co-counselling
Not at all about giving advice, but about being listened to empathically and allowed space to offload heavily charged feelings and re-appraise the life situations which have given rise to them, either in the present or from the past. Two people who have learned the technique of co-counselling (usually on a weekend course) help each other do this on a regular basis, taking it in turns to be the 'counsellor' (i.e., listener/facilitator) or the 'client' (the one talking about whatever is or has been a source of unhappiness in their life). Co-counselling facilitates catharsis (e.g., of grief or anger) in a way that is safe, allows one to stay in charge of the process (in that it is always the 'client' who decides what to talk about), and is free.

For boosting and balancing energy: prophylactic and healing
Acupuncture
Not for you if you pass out at the thought of a needle coming

in contact with your skin! In fact, acupuncture is usually quite painless – and is even sometimes used as an alternative to anaesthesia in surgical operations, especially in China today. At a symposium held in Peking in 1979 by the World Health Organization, a list was compiled by medical acupuncturists from all over the world of diseases they considered amenable to treatment by acupuncture. There were more than forty in all, ranging from asthma and bronchitis, through digestive complaints to migraine, toothache and the common cold.

This ancient Taoist system of healing works directly on energy ('chi') flowing throughout the body in channels called 'meridians'. If this energy is blocked or out of balance, symptoms of 'dis-ease' of some sort may eventually manifest. What an acupuncturist does is to diagnose the imbalance or blockage and then treat it by inserting tiny needles to regulate the energy flow as necessary.

When this is done without needles (by finger or thumb pressure), it is called 'acupressure'. One can learn which points to press to get temporary relief from a whole range of unpleasant symptoms, for example headache or nausea. But, of course, if these persist one should see a doctor.

It is probably true to say that most patients will try acupuncture after more orthodox treatment has failed. But one does not have to wait to be ill before seeking acupuncture. Regular visits to an acupuncturist, like those to the dentist, might well save you pain and trouble later on.

Homoeopathy

The same is also true of homoeopathy. Quite apart from the often quite startling recovery of some sufferers from long-term chronic complaints, homoeopathy is ideal for those times when one is feeling 'off' but has been told by one's GP that he or she can find nothing wrong with us. In the absence of specific symptoms, what shows up in tests or what can be cured by drugs or surgery, allopathic medical practitioners (i.e., doctors) are largely at a loss to help us. A homoeopath might be able to, all depending on whether he or she can find the right remedy. 'Right' means the one (out of hundreds in the *Materia Medica*) that *exactly* matches the energy pattern we manifest. If it doesn't, nothing will happen – which might be boring, but at least, unlike with drugs, there are no side–effects with homoeopathic remedies.

A long time is spent in the initial session on getting a full and accurate picture of the patient's energy state. The questions asked by a homoeopathic practitioner are often unexpected and seemingly quite irrelevant, to do as much with mental and emotional as with physical states: about feelings, preferences, rhythms and life-style. Even more startling is the fact that homoeopathic remedies are so diluted that there may actually be nothing potent remaining in them, yet, if it is the right remedy, it works. And the fact that it works on animals too rules out the placebo effect. Remember that homoeopathy seeks to treat not only physical ailments but negative emotional states as well.

For calming, centering, slowing down

Yoga

The breathing and stretching exercises of yoga are immensely soothing to the nerves when you are under stress. Don't worry – you don't *have* to be able to stand on your head to feel better. Learn the postures either at evening classes or from an illustrated book.

Meditation

(See Chapter 7) Forget the esoteric – just sit, switch off and enjoy your aloneness. It makes you realize (once again) that the only barrier to peace of mind is the mind. If you feel you need some instruction, you could try Transcendental Meditation classes.

T'ai chi

Movement in slow motion. You really do need a teacher for this one. It is also a training in giving one-pointed attention, present-centredness, body awareness and flowing with the energy (as are other martial arts, e.g. Aikido).

For more body awareness and deep relaxation

Massage

An ideal way to get out of your head and back into your body after the day's work and to recharge drained batteries. There are several different types of massage so make sure the person giving the massage knows what you want. You'll get a shock, for example, if you expected a soothing, sensual massage and instead get Shi'atsu (a vigorous and stimulating type of massage-cum-acupressure which could involve you at some stage being literally stood upon by the masseur!). Also, learn how to give yourself a massage when you are feeling tense and drained.

Bathing

Water is a great conductor of energy, and so is very good for changing energy spaces if you are feeling down, negative or stressed. You can swim, shower, take a sauna, or wallow in a hot bath fragrant with oil (preferably by candlelight and with soothing background music). Follow this hydrotherapy (for that is what it is) with a massage or deep relaxation. If you are not going straight to bed afterwards it is always good to put on a fresh set of clothing rather than getting back into the ones carrying stale or negative energy. Doing so will make you feel even more clean and refreshed.

Deep relaxation

Techniques for achieving this vary but what they have in common is that they slow down brain activity from the fast Beta wavelength to the slower Alpha and Theta, which we experience as a blissful, totally relaxed state bordering on sleep. You could take a course in autogenics but it would be cheaper to learn how to switch off your tension at will with the Alpha Plan for complete physical, mental and emotional relaxation described in my *Total Relaxation in Five Steps* (Penguin 1988).

For continued self-development

As one moves out of the Victim Game and into the Energy Game, from coping with what Life lands us with to learning more and more the ways to create the sort of life one wants for oneself, one necessarily gets further into co-operating with one's own process, learning more about who one is and what one is becoming – and the barriers to realizing one's full potential as a creative, free, expressive, caring, *total* human being. Once you're into the game you can't stop it – it goes on for the rest of your life. And why stop it anyway? It's the most fascinating, satisfying, rewarding game in town. Some of the basic ground rules have been outlined in this book. You'll learn more as you go along – and some of them you will have to make up for yourself since your particular way of playing has never been tried before. Your own particular combination of energies is unique, what makes you truly individual.

To help you play the Energy Game better, and maybe to get round the board faster or to help you move on when you temporarily lose your sense of direction, you could try either of the following.

Jungian analysis

Admittedly expensive, but if you can afford it very worthwhile. You will work with your analyst's support towards individuation, reclaiming the parts of yourself lost in the process of your conditioning: projected, rejected, disowned . . . nourishing the seeds of new growth hinted at in your dreams, working with archetypal energies at a very deep level. . . . Too expensive? Then you could have a session or two of . . .

Voice dialogue

A way of understanding and accepting the different subpersonalities within us and how they influence our ways of seeing, feeling, acting and relating. Voice dialogue has the advantage that you can go for one-off sessions when you need them, or learn the technique for yourself in a weekend group which you can then use to hold internal dialogues with the various parts of yourself that are seeking expression rather in the style of the 'active imagination' recommended by Jung. It is a blend of elements, not only of Jung, but also of Gestalt, transactional analysis, psychodrama and meditation. Useful, particularly whenever you feel different energies pulling you different ways, for example, or don't know why you are feeling or behaving the way you are. (See Chapter 9).

The above is only a short list of the resources available to anyone who is taking responsibility for their own health, vitality and peace of mind. It does not include, for example, groups for mutual support and consciousness raising like those geared specifically to the needs of addicts, the disabled, or the bereaved. Neither does it include women's groups or 'Body Positive' groups, or therapies such as the Alexander Technique or reflexology. The point is, that once you decide to take charge of your life, you realize just how much support there is around you and how many potential playmates there are who are willing to share with you the secrets of playing the Energy Game better than you do. By 'better' is meant 'with more awareness' – and the more you learn the art of handling the energies Life presents you from moment to moment in a more conscious way, the more you enjoy the game. And that means you get to enjoy *yourself* more, for the Energy Game is YOU.

Postscript

The possibility that many (if not all) of us could become victims of mishandled energy on a global scale is a recurring concern that affects more and more people today. What is true for us as individuals – that not knowing how to use our own energy creatively makes us victims – is also true collectively. The same laws operate in the macrocosm and the microcosm, the Outer world mirrors the Inner world.

Future historians may well label this age of ours the Nuclear Age, for we have both found that energy is at the heart of matter and learned how to harness it. We have more forms of energy at our disposal, know more about the laws governing it, than any other age before ours. It is a scientific fact that the energy in matter is subtly changed simply by being observed, by the awareness of the observer. Whether we harness energy creatively or destructively depends on the *quality* of the awareness we bring to it. Energy itself is neutral: electricity can inflict horrible burns – or make toast. Satellites can beam the Olympic Games into our living room – or be used by Governments to complete yet another lap in the Arms Race towards Star Wars. We have to know how to use energy, and use it to make life better if it is not to control us, rather than we controlling it. And, when we do use it with a positive intent, with *care*, we do, indeed, improve the quality of our lives. It serves us in its various forms for better health, for less drudgery, for speedier travel, for the greater enjoyment of our leisure.

But there are ominous signs that our level of awareness on a collective level concerning how to deploy the energy resources of our planet is not keeping pace with the cleverness that allowed us to develop them in the first place. There have been too many 'accidents' recently which have created victims on a colossal scale all over the world. What they have in common is that they are the results of either a lack of care or a lack of caring in the energy we are putting out: Bhopal, Tchernobyl, the Rhine ... fractured ozone layers in the atmosphere, polluted oceans, poisoned fish and trees, endangered species ... Mother Earth is long-suffering and compliant: we can venerate her as the giver and sustainer of life – all life – or turn her into a rubbish bin. It's entirely up to us. And never before have the stakes been so high. One of the 'endangered species' may well be our own, unless we meet the challenge of energy turning sour on a global level and starting to manifest as the planet's own equivalent to cancer, stress disease and AIDS. That is, of course, if anybody is left alive to do anything (or indeed, left at all, if our leaders have been so unthinkably unconscious as to unleash the dogs of nuclear war on their fellow men, women and children.

We all need to become more aware of the negative or uncaring energy being beamed out into the world every day: by nations polarizing against each other from motives of power or paranoia; by religious sects more intent on spreading a gospel of hatred and division than of love and universality; by the media (for whom all news seems to be bad news) which serve up stories of disaster, horror and violence for our daily entertainment. We become victims of their thought-forms, the view of reality they are projecting – and get used to seeing the world as a jungle fraught with danger where it is every man for himself. And if the model inside our heads is that of a jungle, it will become one – or rather, we will make it one. Perception is selective, and we will filter out from our awareness anything that does not fit into what we are geared to see. We get the world we create, and we have the power to create heaven or hell right here on Earth, for they are nothing but states of mind from which forms manifest.

All credit is due to those who are already working to create
a cleaner, freer, more human and humane world. Some are
putting out positive energy in the areas of human rights,
others towards conservation, yet others towards peace or to
working for the Third World. In fact, there is only One World,
in which two thirds are victims of the Idea of Scarcity that
causes the other third to hoard rather than to trust in the idea
of Abundance and to make it a reality for everybody alive on
this abundant planet. That ideas can be changed on a global
level was witnessed by one of the most beautiful phenomena
in history, the Live Aid concert when, for a day, awareness
and compassion beamed all over the world from satellites in
the sky. Even the sun seemed to shine more brightly that day,
and the world seemed indeed a lighter place. But it was *us*
who made it so for this 'one brief shining moment', for, as the
song acknowledged, 'We are the World'.

Alas, too often, when a light is lit somewhere in the world it
is too soon snuffed out: from Gandhi to Martin Luther King,
from Pope John to John Lennon ... And yet, perhaps, not
before the flame of a new awareness, a new way of seeing, has
been kindled in those who loved and mourn them. Anyone
who has charisma, or is in a position of influence or power,
bears a tremendous responsibility for the energy they channel
into the world, leaving it a lighter or a heavier place. We may
not all be Mother Teresas and, fortunately, it is given to few
to be like Hitler. But, for each of we 'ordinary' people, in our
own little way, the energy we choose to put out, adds to the
sum total of positive or negative energy at any one time in the
world. One choice we have is to collude with the darker
energies in this world and make it an even darker place by
adding our own brand of negativity. But if, stopping the Victim
Game, we work on our own energy, at being more positive, at
creating a different reality by being 'a light unto ourselves',
there is a good chance that the flame of awareness will be
kindled too in others with whom we come in contact: our
families and friends, people we work with. For when others
see that you have 'lightened up', have stopped giving yourself a hard time, they too may be encouraged to start taking
charge of their own lives. Awareness is catching. If enough

of us spread it around we could, hopefully, have a world
epidemic.

> The best of happiness,
> Honour and fortunes, keep with you!

Timon of Athens (I.ii)

Grumbling appendix
(Victims' letters to the author)

Dear Lewis Proctor,
Balderdash and poppycock! If everybody behaved the way you
advise us to in your book, what sort of world would this be? I
think it would be **awful**, because we would all become very
selfish, doing what we wanted all the time instead of doing The
Right Thing. What about duty, obligation, stiff upper lip and
all that? It's what made this country great, when everyone knew
their place and did not get ideas above their station. And
what's all this about being 'suffocated' by the Old School Tie?
At least, in **my** school, we were given a jolly good hiding
whenever we stepped out of line – and it did **me** no harm at all,
as you can see. Are you some sort of long-haired hippy or
something?

Outraged,
Belgravia.

Dear Louie Proot,
How could you? As if things are not bad enough already, you
blame us in your silly little book for making them worse ourselves. I think you must be a cruel person to say such things. If
you only knew what I have had to put up with in my life you
would not write such horrible things and hurt other people so
much. But then, I'm used to this sort of thing, and have had to

put up with it all my life. Nobody has any consideration these days.

Marta,
Weston-super-Mare

Dear Louise Prout,
You have got it all wrong. The Bible is very clear in its teaching that we are in this world to suffer for our sins. Why else would God punish people with AIDS unless they deserved it for the sexual way a lot of them have been behaving recently (especially perverts)? Also, you are wrong to blame Adam. If you take the trouble to read the Book of Genesis properly you will see that it was all Eve's fault in the first place. But then, what can you expect from a woman?

Jeremiah,
Peckham

Dear Author (I've forgotten your name),
I hope your publishers have passed this letter on to you, together with my strongest protests about the dangerous ideas contained in your book. I decided to burn it in the garden so that my family should not get to read it. I do not want my husband to get any funny ideas about doing what he wants to do rather than keeping the peace. He might even decide one night for a change not to wash up after cooking the dinner and go off to the pub on his own, Heaven forbid! My children also need protecting against your new-fangled ideas. Do you think I want my son to think he can drop out of his accountant's training to go to art school? He has to think of his future and train for a sensible job. Did you ever stop to think how I would feel if my teenage daughter started staying out at night? I think 10.30 is late enough already, don't you? Obviously you don't, and have no respect at all for the sanctity of family life.

Furious,
Surbiton.

By the same author

Who's Pulling Your Strings?

Have you ever wondered why you act the way you do? Why, for example, did you choose your career, your husband, your wife or your lover? Why do you vote the way you do, have the dreams you do, attract the experiences you do?

Of course, it isn't just coincidence. What we call our 'character' or our 'nature' is a mixture of different personalities, but because we are unaware of them we let them control us. Our Inner Critic, for example, tries to tell us we're not good enough, our Pleaser often makes us do things we shouldn't just to keep others happy, and our Wanderer can make us feel restless and unchallenged. When one personality pulls a string we get angry, when another tugs a string we get jealous, anxious or embarrassed.

Yet all of these personalities are essential because they are part of what we are. Using some of the techniques and theories of psychotherapy, **Louis Proto** shows how we can balance these personalities to control how we feel and how we react. You can then explore your own character and learn to pull your own strings.

Coming Alive

Wake up feeling *good* every day of your life. This is the invitation **Louis Proto** extends to us all in this unique do-it-yourself manual for coming alive spiritually, mentally and physically. The emphasis throughout is on practical exercises and techniques that can be fitted into even the busiest of daily routines yet *do* bring real and lasting beneficial results. He discusses in an easy and informal manner:

- Throwing out negativity
- Body awareness
- Diet and relaxation
- Meditation

- Self diagnosis
- Creative visualization
- Yoga and reflexology
- Massage

Of further interest

The Calm Technique

Simple meditation techniques that really work

Using a straightforward and infectious writing style **Paul Wilson** explains how meditation can both calm and refresh you. No religious ritual, no deep mysticism, just a simple daily routine that will:

- Ease stress and help you cope better
- Improve your eating habits . . . and your sex life!
- Create self confidence and renewed vigour
- Reduce the effects of ageing
- Make you look - and feel - years younger

All you need is between 30 and 60 minutes a day regular application to radically improve *your* life in every conceivable direction.

WHO'S PULLING YOUR STRINGS	0 7225 2870 1	£5.99	☐
COMING ALIVE	0 7225 2419 6	£3.99	☐
THE CALM TECHNIQUE	0 7225 1468 9	£4.99	☐
HOW TO READ A PERSON LIKE A BOOK	0 7225 1120 5	£5.99	☐
MANAGING ANGER	0 7225 2715 2	£5.99	☐
HOW TO DEVELOP A SUPER-POWER MEMORY	0 7225 2784 5	£3.99	☐
TOO PERFECT	0 7225 2786 1	£6.99	☐
WEALTH 101	0 7225 2855 8	£8.99	☐

All these books are available from your local bookseller or can be ordered direct from the publishers.

To order direct just tick the titles you want and fill in the form below:

Name: _____

Address: _____

_____

_____ Postcode: _____

Send to: Thorsons Mail Order, Dept 3, HarperCollins*Publishers*, Westerhill Road, Bishopbriggs, Glasgow G64 2QT.
Please enclose a cheque or postal order or your authority to debit your Visa/Access account —

Credit card no: ☐☐☐☐☐☐☐☐☐☐☐☐☐☐☐☐

Expiry date: _____

Signature: _____

— to the value of the cover price plus:
UK & BFPO: Add £1.00 for the first book and 25p for each additional book ordered.
Overseas orders including Eire: Please add £2.95 service charge. Books will be sent by surface mail but quotes for airmail despatches will be given on request.
24 HOUR TELEPHONE ORDERING SERVICE FOR ACCESS/VISA CARDHOLDERS — TEL: 041 772 2281.